MARIE SMITH

The Book of Life

The Lamb of God

John 3: 16

"For God so loved the world, that he gave his only begotten Son, that whosoever believeth in him should not perish, but have everlasting life."

ARPress

ARPress
45 Dan Road Suite 5
Canton MA 02021

Hotline: 1(888) 821-0229
Fax: 1(508) 545-7580

Ordering Information:

Quantity sales. Special discounts are available on quantity purchases by corporations, associations, and others. For details, contact the publisher at the address above.

Printed in the United States of America.

ISBN-13:   Softcover   979-8-89389-302-1
                eBook   979-8-89389-303-8
Library of Congress Control Number: 2024915201

TO THE GLORY OF GOD

TABLE OF CONTENTS

The Book of Revelation

We are in the last days at a time when violence, murder, homosexuality, sexual immorality, human trafficking, sodomite, and false teaching. When evil and uncertainty is very much in our sight and growing daily. The world is looking for answers and some Christians are looking for encouragement to know who God is and strengthen their faith in the Lord. Many Christians and unsaved humanity don't know about the book of Revelation, and it purpose in the greater schemes of things that is happening. In my book, I draw upon years of biblical study and research to shed some light on a subject that is close and dear to the Lord heart for souls. We can see in the Book of Revelation many warnings throughout the book; there are many movies about the history and stories of the Seven Churches. What about the warnings and danger of the sins and no repentance of humanity in these churches and where their final destination will be. The Book of Life is for the saved and The Book of Damnation is for the unsaved.

There is no longer A Fear of God!

And do not fear those who kill the body but cannot kill the soul. But rather fear him (Jesus) who can destroy both soul and body in hell. (Matthew 10: 28).

The road to Hell is paved with the bones of priests and monks, and the skulls of Bishops are the lamp posts that light the path.

The road to hell is paved with the skulls of erring priests, with bishops as their signposts. **(St. John Chrysostom, extract from St. John Chrysostom, Homily III on Acts 1:12)**

WARNING

My book: **The Angels of the Seven Churches**: is a **Warning** to Humanity, and All Nations, World Leaders, State, City, County, All Civil Officials, Shepherds and Five-Fold Ministries, and Churches.

The Lord gave me a **Vision of Hell**:

I had a vision where the angel of the Lord took me to heaven and Jesus. Jesus took my hand and spoke, do not let go of my hand no matter what you see. Then he waved his hand, the veil lifted, we went down the steps, and I saw a giant demon and many people rows after rows; you could not count. I asked the Lord who is all these people, and Jesus answered, "these are my shepherds that have led my flock astray", I asked him if any of the shepherds made it into heaven because it looked like trillions of shepherds in hell. He did not answer. Jesus waves his hand and uncovers some shepherd's faces; some I knew, some I did not realize until later.

Then he showed a mighty teacher in the word of God I knew in a caged crying; she said, "I thought they were teaching me right". Then Jesus said, did you ask me if they are teaching you right; she said "No" and started to cry; He said, "Judgment has been set!" I did not feel the heat in hell nor hear their screams or torture of the people.

Then Jesus told me to write this book: The Angels of The Seven Churches. The world leaders, shepherds, and the churches are asleep and need to wake up! Then fix themselves and take to the Lord in Prayer.

1. The World leaders, State, County, and City Officials, Shepherds, and Churches:

Isaiah 9:16 For the leaders of these peoples cause them to err, and those they lead are destroyed.

2. Christian Witches:

1 Samuel 15: 23 For rebellion is the sin of witchcraft, and stubbornness is iniquity and idolatry. Because you have rejected the Word of the Lord, He also has rejected you from being king.

3. Irresponsible Shepherds: Ezekiel 34:1-10,

Ezekiel Chapter 34:1-10

Ezekiel 34:1 "**And the word of the LORD came unto me, saying,**"

It is against a brand-new prophecy. Ezekiel turns from the people to their leaders, who have the most significant guilt.

From this chapter on, Ezekiel's messages are primarily comforting, telling of God's grace and faithfulness to His covenant promises.

Ezekiel 34:2 "Son of man, prophesy against the shepherds of Israel, prophesy, and say unto them, thus saith the Lord GOD unto the shepherds; Woe be to the shepherds of Israel that do feed themselves! Should not the shepherds feed the flocks?"

"Prophesy against the shepherds of Israel": The reference was to pre-exilic leaders such as kings, priests, and prophets - their civil leaders, as well as their spiritual leaders, which means those false ones who fleeced the flock for personal gain (verses 3-4), rather than fed or led righteously. It stands in contrast to the Lord as Shepherd.

These Scriptures also have a meaning for the Jews and Christians. We will try to look at both as we go along. These verses' beginning is a reprimand for not caring for the sheep. The kings and preachers must now be careful in feeding the sheep. That is the primary job of a shepherd.

<u>Ezekiel 34:3</u> "Ye eat the fat, and ye clothe you with the wool, ye kill them that are fed, but ye feed not the flock."

It speaks of those who take from the sheep and give nothing. We see in some churches today that ministers are living far above the conditions of their people and are not teaching them true doctrine or the dangers of not living according to God's Holy Word.

<u>Ezekiel 34:4</u> "The diseased have ye not strengthened, neither have ye healed that which was sick, neither have ye bound up [that which was] broken, neither have ye brought again that which were driven away, neither have ye sought that which was lost; but with force and with cruelty have ye ruled them."

Some treat the church as a hotel for saints and not a hospital for sinners.

<u>Mark 2:17</u> "When Jesus heard it, he saith unto them, They that are whole have no need of the physician, but they that are sick: I came not to call the righteous, but sinners to repentance."

Those whose spirits are sick need us. The weak sheep need more care than the healthy ones. A good shepherd keeps his sheep together with love, patience, and kindness, not by driving them. Jesus told the parable about the Shepherd that left the 99 and went to find the one that lost. The 23rd Psalm describes the good Shepherd.

<u>Ezekiel 34:5</u> "And they were scattered because there is no shepherd: and they became meat to all the beasts of the field when they were scattered."

When the flock is divided, it is easy prey for the wolves. They get one sheep off from the others and kill him. It is true of the church. Together we stand; divided, we fall. The wolf is not afraid of the sheep but scared of the Shepherd. The Shepherd drives the wolf away and saves the sheep.

In verse above, there is no shepherd. The sheep are easy prey. Therefore, a Christian needs fellowship in a church with other Christians and to be under the care of a pastor. There is safety in the numbers, and the pastor protects the single member. The pastor is a protector and guide.

The beasts of the field pictured here picture the nations that prey on Israel (Dan. 7:3-7), though it could include actual wild beasts (as in 14:21, 34:25, and 28).

Ezekiel 34:6 "My sheep wandered through all the mountains, and upon every high hill: yea, my flock was scattered upon all the face of the earth, and none did search or seek after them."

Holding a civil office or an office in a church carries a grave responsibility. We should not take office if we have not weighed the cost and are willing to sacrifice to do a good job. The loss of the world today is like those sheep in the mountains. We must go and get them.

To be saved yourself is excellent, but God called His workers to seek out the lost. How can they be saved without hearing? They must listen to the Word of God to be saved.

Ezekiel 34:7 "Therefore, ye shepherds, hear the word of the LORD."

It is not just an idle statement but a warning to the ministers of today and the leaders of the Jews then.

Ezekiel 34:8 "As I live, saith the Lord GOD, surely because my flock became a prey, and my flock became meat to every beast of the field because there was no shepherd, neither did my shepherds search for my flock, but the shepherds fed themselves, and fed not my flock;"

All who work in the ministry should be ministering because God called them to that task, not as a way of making a living. Of course, you must have a living, but it should not be your reason for accepting a specific job.

The food that the minister of God must bring the flock is the pure Word of God. The Word cannot be watered down, or it will not nourish the sheep. The sheep will not be in danger of straying away when they are well-fed. When they know the Word of God, they are not as quickly drawn away to false prophets.

<u>Ezekiel 34:9</u> "Therefore, O ye shepherds, hear the word of the LORD;"

It is no idle threat, as proven by the case of King Zedekiah (<u>Jer. 52:10-11</u>).

<u>Ezekiel 34:10</u> "Thus saith the Lord GOD; Behold, I am against the shepherds; and I will require my flock at their hand and cause them to cease from feeding the flock; neither shall the shepherds feed themselves anymore; for I will deliver my flock from their mouth, that they may not be meat for them."

God will not allow a leader to go on who does not care for the people. These shepherds, who do not care for the sheep, will be replaced by someone who cares for the sheep. The owner (God) does not want to lose his sheep. The critical Word in the verse above is a mouth full. He will deliver them from his mouth.

Angels of the Seven Churches

The mystery of the seven stars you saw in my right hand and the seven golden lampstands.

The Seven Stars: are the angels of the seven churches, and

The Seven Lampstands: which you saw, are the seven churches (Rev. 1:20).

Revelation 2:

To the angel of the church of Ephesus, write, The Loveless Church:

Nevertheless, I have this against you, that you have left your first love. Remember, therefore, from where you have fallen, repent and do the first works, or else I will come to you quickly and remove your lampstand from its place -unless you repent. To him who overcomes, I will give to eat from the Tree of Life, which is amid the paradise of God.

Let him hear what the Spirit says to the churches who have an ear. (Holy Bible, KJV, 2012).

To the angel of the church in Smyrna writes, The Persecuted Church:

I know the blasphemy of those who say they are Jews and are not but are a synagogue of Satan. Do not fear any of those things which you are about to suffer. Indeed, the devil is about to throw some of you into prison, that you may be tested, and you will have tribulation for ten days. Be faithful until death, and I will give the crown of life. The second death shall not hurt him who overcomes.

Let him hear what the Spirit says to the churches who have an ear. (Holy Bible, KJV, 2012).

To the church's angel in Pergamos write, The Compromising Church:

I know your works, where you dwell, where Satan's throne is. But I have a few things against you because you have; they're those who hold the doctrine of Balaam, who taught Balak to put a stumbling block before the children of Israel, to eat things sacrificed to idols, and commit sexual immorality. Repent, or else I will come to you quickly and fight against them with the sword of my mouth. Let him hear what the Spirit says to the churches who have an ear. To him who overcomes, I will give him a Whitestone and a new name written on the stone that no one knows except him who receives it.

Let him hear what the Spirit says to the churches who have an ear. (Holy Bible, KJV, 2012).

To the church's angel in Thyatira, write The Corrupt Church:

Nevertheless, I have a few things against you because you allow that woman Jezebel, who calls herself prophetess, to teach and seduce my servants to commit sexual immorality and eat things sacrificed to idols. And I gave her time to repent of her sexual sin, and she did not repent. I will cast her into a sickbed and those who commit adultery with her into great tribulation unless they repent of their deed.

Let him hear what the Spirit says to the churches who have an ear. (Holy Bible, KJV, 2012).

Revelation 3:

To the angel of the church in Sardis, write The Dead Church:

Remember therefore how you have received and heard; hold fast and repent, therefore, if you do not watch, I will come upon you as a thief, and you will not know what hour I will come upon you. You have a few names even in Sardis who have not defiled their garments, and they shall walk with Me in white, for they are worthy. He who comes shall be clothed in white garments, and I will not blot out his name from the Book of Life, but I will confess his name before My Father and before His angels.

Let him hear what the Spirit says to the churches who have an ear. (Holy Bible, KJV, 2012).

To the church's angel in Philadelphia, write, The Faithful Church:

Behold, I am coming quickly! Hold fast what you have, that no one may take your crown. He who overcomes, I will make him a pillar in the temple of My God, and he shall go out no more. I will write on him the name of My God and the name of the city of My God, the New Jerusalem, which comes down out of heaven from My God. And I will Write Him My new name.

Let him hear what the Spirit says to the churches who have an ear. (Holy Bible, KJV, 2012).

To the angel of the church of the Laodiceans write, The Lukewarm Church:

Because you say, I am rich, have become wealthy, and need nothing- and do not know that you are wretched, miserable, poor, blind and naked- I counsel you to buy from Me gold refined in the fire, that you may be rich; and white garments, that you may be clothed, that the shame of your nakedness may not be revealed; and anoint your eyes with eye salve, that you may see. As many as I love, I rebuke and chasten. Behold, I stand at the door and knock. If anyone hears My voice and opens the door, I will come into him and dine with him, and he with Me. I will grant to sit with Me on My Throne to him who overcomes, as I also overcame and sat down with My Father on His throne.

Let him hear what the Spirit says to the churches who have an ear. (Holy Bible, KJV, 2012).

References:

KJV, The Holy Bible, (2012). (ALL RIGHTS RESERVED). The Holy Bible KJV. Knoxville, TN 37921: Power Publishing Corporation.

NKJV, The Holy Bible, (2012). Spiritual Warfare Bible. Lake Mary, Florida 32746: Charisma House.

Unknown. (12th Century). Old and New Testaments. Rome: Canonical Books.

Introduction

The Bible is the inspired, unfailing Word of God. The Bible has the mind of God, the state of man, the way to salvation, the doom of sinners, and the happiness of believers. Its principles are holy, its teachings are binding, its histories are actual, its prophecies are correct, and its decisions are complete.

Jesus Christ gave us the eight Beatitudes in the Sermon on the Mount, recorded for all posterity in the Gospel of Matthew, the first book of the New Testament. Matthew's Gospel to an audience steeped in Hebrew tradition. The Gospel of Matthew stresses that Jesus Christ is the Messiah foretold in Hebrew Scripture, our Old Testament, and that the Kingdom of the Messiah is the Kingdom of God in Heaven. Jesus offers us a way of life that promises eternity in Heaven's kingdom.

The teachings of Christ Jesus were simple but unique and innovative at the time of his life on earth. He began teaching about 30 ADS during the ruthless Roman occupation of Palestine. At the time, there were four major Jewish groups: the Pharisees, Sadducees, Essenes, and the Zealots, all of whom presented a different viewpoint to the Jewish people. The Pharisees demanded strict observance of the Mosaic Law expressed in the Torah but also accepted the oral tradition of Jewish customs and rituals. The Sadducees were mainly from priestly families and strictly accepted the Law of Moses but rejected oral tradition.

The Pharisees, unlike the Sadducees, believed in the resurrection of the dead. The monastic Essenes awaited a Messiah to set up a Kingdom on earth and free the Israelites from oppression. The Zealots were a militant Jewish group who wanted freedom for their homeland and centered in Galilee; one of the Twelve Apostles was Simon the Zealot.

The Ten Commandments, given to Moses on Mount Sinai in the Old Testament Book of Exodus, related a series of Thou shalt not phrases, evils one must avoid daily on earth.

Jesus's message is humility, charity, and brotherly love. He teaches the transformation of the inner person. Jesus presents the Beatitudes positively, virtues that will ultimately lead to reward. Love becomes the motivation for the Christian. All the beatitudes have an eschatological meaning; they promise salvation- not in this world, but in the next.

The Beatitudes start one of Matthew's Gospel's central themes: the Kingdom so long awaited in the Old Testament is not of this world but of the next, the Kingdom of Heaven. While the Beatitudes of Jesus offer a way of life that promises salvation, they also offer peace during our trials and tribulations.

John 3:16 "For God so loved the world, that he gave his only begotten Son, that whosoever believeth in him should not perish, but have everlasting life."

It is the most quoted Scripture in the entire Bible. You can easily see why because it is full of so much hope. We need to take a very good look at it. "God so loved"; this is a love so far above anything man knows that we do not understand.

The word love here is translated from Agape which means to love much in a moral sense. This love goes way beyond the human ability to love. This type of love is not because, but despite. He loved us with this love so much, that while we were yet in sin, He sent His Son to die on the cross to save us: not because we deserved it, but because we didn't deserve it.

The Son's mission is bound up in the supreme love of God for the evil, sinful "world" of humanity that is in rebellion against Him. The word "so" emphasizes the intensity or greatness of His love. The Father gave His unique and beloved Son to die on behalf of sinful men.

Jesus came to save the lost. It is so simple and yet so hard. Believeth here again, means continues to believe. You see, salvation is a way of life. Every day when we get up, we must remember all over again and believe. This is not something we do casually. This belief means to believe in God and love Him more than anything or anyone else.

Matthew 22:37 tells us what this love and belief is: "Jesus said unto him, thou shalt love the Lord thy God, with all thy heart, and with all thy soul, and with all thy mind."

You see, if you believe, you will walk holy. God will be first in your life, or He will not be in your life at all. There is no way to perish if you are in the right standing with God. He has prepared for us a place to spend all of eternity with Him.

John 3:17 "For God sent not his Son into the world to condemn the world; but that the world through him might be saved."

This "*sent here*" shows that Jesus is on a mission to carry out His work forever. The name Jesus, as we have said before, means Savior or Jehovah Savior. The Word took on the name of Jesus Christ for His work of salvation. There is a time, at the end of the age, when Jesus will be the Judge and will decide each of our destinations, whether heaven or hell.

His mission to the earth, however, was to save all mankind who would accept it. The name of Jesus is very powerful. The only way to get to heaven is through belief in Him. So, through Him, we receive eternal life.

John 3:18 "He that believeth on him is not condemned: but he that believeth not is condemned already, because he hath not believed in the name of the only begotten Son of God."

Salvation is so simple. So many do not receive God, because they have pre-conceived ideas of how it is so hard to be saved. Faith in the name of Jesus Christ, speaking of this belief to others, and a love for God that surpasses all others are so intertwined that they are inseparable. To believe in Him truly and completely changes our life.

This phrase literally "*to believe in him*", means more than mere intellectual ascent to the claims of the gospel. It includes trust and commitment to Christ as Lord and Savior which results in receiving a new nature, which produces a change in heart and obedience to the Lord.

To believe in the name of Jesus causes us to keep His commandments. To believe in His name brings peace, joy, and hope. If we believe, we are confident of the resurrection.

We are not like those who have refused Him and have no hope. When Thomas asked Jesus how he could know the way, Jesus said *"I am the Way, the Truth, and the Life."*

John 3:19 "And this is the condemnation, that light is come into the world, and men loved darkness rather than light, because their deeds were evil."

We have spoken so much about the Light. The Light is Jesus. The Light gives everything the power to live. The best thing this Light does is do away with darkness. The great thing about this Light is that it shines into all the corners of life and makes manifest visible, the works.

People, who have rejected the Light of Jesus, want their deeds to be hidden by darkness. They are ashamed to have them out in the open. I have said it before, but notice most crimes are done under cover of darkness. Where light is absent, darkness prevails.

Everything about darkness pertains to Satan and his crowd. Come to the Light and let this Light do away with all the darkness in your life.

John 3:20 "For everyone that doe evil hated the light, neither comes to the light, lest his deeds should be reproved."

We see here a difference. The evildoer will hate the Light because it would reveal his evil conduct. It has to do with the followers of Jesus Light, and the followers of Satan's darkness.

Those who drink, swear, and do all sorts of bad things hate those who do good things. It gives the evil children of darkness a terrible guilt complex to be around those of truth and life. Judgments are bound to come up, and those who walk in darkness fall way short.

Those who are living evil lives hate those who are following Jesus. Their sins make them feel guilty, and that causes them to hate.

John 3:21 "But he that doe truth come to the light, that his deeds may be made manifest, that they are wrought in God."

Truth, love, joy, peace, honesty, and happiness need no darkness to hide in. They are harvests of the Light. Those who live in the Light are eager to have any small things in their life that are not pleasing to God become known to them, so they can get rid of them.

They are growing constantly in honesty, peace, and truth. The Light reveals what is there. If they are good deeds, you do not want them hidden.

Chapter 1

The Kingdom of Heaven

Jesus began with the Beatitudes, describing the character and blessedness of those who would be citizens of the kingdom and illustrating their relation to the world as salt and light. Clarifying his relationship with the Law, Jesus stressed how our righteousness must surpass that of the Scribes and Pharisees.

The beatitudes come from the opening verses of the famous Sermon on the Mount delivered by Jesus and recorded in Matthew 5:3-12. Here, Jesus states several blessings, each beginning with the phrase, Blessed are declarations appear in Jesus Sermon Luke 6: 20-23. Each saying speaks of a gift or divine favor bestowed upon a person for owning a particular character quality.

The word beatitude comes from the Latin beatitude, meaning blessedness. The Phrase blessed in each of the beatitudes implies a current state of happiness or well-being. The expression gave the day's people a powerful meaning of divine joy and perfect happiness. In other words, Jesus was saying divinely happy and fortunate are those who have these inward qualities. While speaking of a current blessedness, a promise of a future reward.

Revelation 4:1-5

Verses 4:1 – 5:14: The third significant section of Revelation begins here: "the things which shall be hereafter" (1:19). Chapters four and five set up Christ's right and authority to act as the Judge of the earth. God on His throne invests the Lion of the tribe of Judah with the power to set up His dominion and kingdom on earth because of His redeeming work as the Lamb.

Revelation 4:1: "After this, I looked, and behold a door [was] opened in heaven: and the first voice which I heard was as it were of a trumpet talking with me, which said, come up hither, and I will show thee things which must be hereafter."

The door signifies entrance by way of revelation into heaven. The command "Come up hither probably does not refer specifically to the Rapture but rather to the change in the scene for John, who will receive revelation about future events. The book's final section describes the events that follow the church age.

The phrases *"after this"* and "things which must be hereafter" move to the future, beyond the age of the church. The "door" signifies entrance by way of revelation into heaven. Chapters four and five picture a heavenly scene. The *"trumpet"* is an authoritative voice.

Matthew 24:31: "And he shall send his angels with a great sound of a trumpet, and they shall gather together his elect from the four winds, from one end of heaven to the other."

All the elects are gathered and assembled before Christ. It is the height of world history, ushering in the millennial reign of Christ.

It will be the trumpet of assembly *the silver trumpet of redemption*, *"four"* (Matthew 24:31) means the entire world. We've all heard the saying: "From the four corners of the earth, I'm sure. This assembly will not be just Americans, but the true believers from every country of the world. These "angels" are ministering spirits who carry out these orders of their Lord and Master. *The "He" here is Jesus Messiah,* but now He is Lord of lords and King of kings.

It *"sound of a Trumpet"* could be a literal trumpet blowing or the voice of our Lord sounding like a trumpet. This is the last chronological mention of silver in the Bible. There will be no silver in heaven.

"Silver" means redemption, and there is no silver there because we have already been redeemed. There is only gold in heaven. In the Holy of Holies, there was only gold, because in the presence of God, there was only gold. This gathering together of His elect is commonly

referred to as the church's rapture. His church has no denomination. It is "all" who truly believe in the Lord Jesus Christ.

1 Corinthians: "In a moment, in the twinkling of an eye, at the last trump: for the trumpet shall sound, and the dead shall be raised incorruptible, and we shall be changed."

1 Thessalonians 4:16-17 "For the Lord himself shall descend from heaven with a shout, with the voice of the archangel, and with the trump of God: and the dead in Christ shall rise first:" "Then we which are alive [and] remain shall be caught up together with them in the clouds, to meet the Lord in the air: and so shall we ever be with the Lord."

To understand, read all this account. I have chosen just two verses from the account for here. This will happen so quickly that you will not even have time to blink your eye.

The *"I"* (in verse 1), is of course John who is writing this. Jesus has been speaking in the earlier chapter directly. Now we hear from John about the things he saw. It is after Jesus finishes His messages to the seven churches.

We will see the number "*seven*" throughout Revelation. *Seven: means "spiritually complete"*. Perhaps in this number, God is saying, this is it. There is nothing else to read. If you can't get the message in Revelation, you cannot receive it.

John looks toward heaven and is startled *"Behold"; the door of heaven is open.* Jesus is the door to heaven. The door of heaven is not closed to the believers in the Lord Jesus Christ. Jesus opened the way to the very throne of God when the temple curtain was torn from the top to the bottom (opening the way to the holy of holies) when He died on the cross (Matthew 27:51).

The word "looked" is important also. We must look for it before we can find it. Jesus is coming back for those who are looking for Him.

Notice, this door was "opened" in the past tense. It is not going to be opened. Jesus opened it for us. It is now open to believers.

John 10:7 "Then said Jesus unto them again, Verily, verily, I say unto you, I am the door of the sheep."

Heaven is presently the dwelling place of God. It will also be our eternal home.

The first voice that John hears is either the voice of Jesus Himself or the voice of Jesus' messenger. It makes no difference, the message itself is from Jesus.

There are several other instances in the Bible where the door of heaven was opened. Many prophets also have seen a vision of the heavenly.

Ezekiel speaks of his look into heaven. Daniel had a glimpse into heaven. When Stephen was stoned to death, he saw into heaven.

When Stephen investigated heaven, he saw Jesus standing at the right hand of God. Most times, Jesus is seated at the right hand because His work is completed, but I believe that He was standing to receive His faithful servant, Stephen, home.

This door has never been closed to the true believers.

The first voice that John hears (in verse 1), is either the voice of Jesus Himself or the voice of Jesus' messenger. It makes no difference; the message itself is from Jesus. When the Lord calls us to meet Him in the air, when the church is caught away, we will hear the trumpet, the silver trumpet of redemption.

In Both *(Matthew 24:31 and 1 Thessalonians 4:16),* I read at first the voice and the trumpet seem interchangeable. The voices of Jesus and His angels are also a little confusing. Either way, the message is from Jesus. This trumpet was talking with John.

The voice that John heard was like a trumpet. This is a powerful voice; it gives an authentic sound. This voice is talking to us, as well as John.

The voice said, *"Come up hither"* to John, but is always saying to us, *"Come up hither".* Get your mind off the things of this world and look heavenward. The call of Jesus has always been *"Come".* In this specific sentence, He tells John "Come up hither", then adds why.

Jesus, the voice, says, "I will show thee things which must be hereafter." John will be shown a look into the future. John could have had a vision of this, or he could have been transported into heaven for a moment in time to see all of this. We know that viewing something from the earth makes us see the here and now. From a heavenly point, we can see yesterday and tomorrow.

Notice that these things of the hereafter must be. Why must they be? Because God ordered it from the beginning of the world and God never changes. We must change to fit His plan, not the other way around.

John is not told a specific time in the hereafter, only that it will be later than the present time he is in.

John is now seeing into the future, after the believers in Christ are raptured into heaven, in this scene.

Verses 2-5: "In the spirit": John sees God the Father sitting on His *"throne"* in "heaven", (verse 8). The gems and the "rainbow" show the glory of God (Ezek. 1:22-28). The *twenty-four "elders"* probably represent the raptured church in heaven.

Their *"seats" or thrones* show a reward of authority in the millennial kingdom (compare 20:4), and their "crowns" (Greek Stephanos), are crowns of reward from the judgment seat of Christ (Rom. 14:10; 1 Cor. 3:12-15; 2 Cor. 5:10). The *"white raiment"* shows their righteousness, which has now been judged and purified. The number "four and twenty", represents the church as priests before God. David divided the Levitical priesthood into twenty- four sections (1 Chron. 24:7-19). Believers are seen here as a kingdom of priests (1:6). Old Testament saints are not yet included, since they will not be resurrected and rewarded until after the Tribulation period (Dan. 12:1-3). The "seven lamps" or *"seven spirits"*: again, symbolize the Holy Spirit of God (Rev.1:4).

Revelation 4:2 "And immediately I was in the spirit: and behold, a throne was set in heaven, and one sat on the throne."

John was already in the Spirit we know from an earlier lesson, but this means a deeper experience in the Spirit. A double dose of the Spirit, you might say.

"Throne": Not so much a piece of furniture, but a symbol of sovereign rule and authority (7:15; 11:19; 16:17-18; Isa. 6:1). It is the focus (of chapter 4), occurring 13 times, 11 times referring to God's throne.

John was changed or transported, instantly. This throne, as we said before, has been seen by many in the Bible. The word "one" does not mean "one" but, I believe it means the unity of the trinity.

(1)   God the Father.

(2)   God the Son or God the Word.

(3)   God the Holy Spirit.

A throne shows rulership and power. Notice that the "*throne*" was "*set in heaven*"; the set is past tense. This throne is occupied even now in heaven, where Jesus sits at the right hand of the Father.

Revelation 4:3 "And he that sat was to look upon like a jasper and a sardine stone: and there was a rainbow round about the throne, in sight like unto an emerald."

The "*jasper and sardine stones*" were the most precious of all stones. The beauty of God was so dazzling that John could not describe Him. The jasper was the last and the sardine the first stone in the breastplate worn by the High Priest (Exodus 28:17-20). These stones are in the foundation of the new Jerusalem (Revelation 21:19-20).

The diamond and ruby are meant by these stones. These stones are known for their clearness and brightness.

There was a diamond between the breastplate and the heart of the high priest. The name engraved on this stone, I believe, is the unspeakable name of God Almighty. The diamond stone next to the heart stood for purity and mercy.

The *emerald is another precious stone, green in color.* Green means "*earthly or of the earth".* The emerald was also part of the breastplate and of the foundation of New Jerusalem.

The value of these three different stones is greater than other stones. These are classified as precious stones and are very expensive.

This rainbow is green (earthly), to show the covenant between God and man. The first rainbow mentioned was a sign of a promise from God to man. God would never again destroy the earth by water. Sometimes it is called a bow, and sometimes a rainbow. The rainbow encircles the throne as a constant reminder to God and man of the covenant. This is a beautiful sight to behold.

Revelation 4:4 "And round about the throne were four and twenty seats: and upon the seats I saw four and twenty elders sitting, clothed in white raiment; and they had on their heads crowns of gold."

The *"four and twenty seats"* were thrones. Miniature thrones in authority, are subordinate to God, but they surround the throne of God.

"Four and twenty elders": Their joint rule with Christ, their white garments, and their golden crowns all seem to show that these 24 represent the redeemed (verses 9:11; 5:5-14; 7:11-17; 11:16-18; 14:3; 19:4). The question is which redeemed? Not Israel, since the nation is not yet saved, glorified, and coronated.

That is still to come at this point in the events of the end. Their resurrection and glory will come at the end of the seven-year tribulation time (Dan. 12:1-3). Tribulation saints aren't yet saved (7:9-10). Only one group will be complete and glorified at that point, the church. Here elders are the church, which sings the song of redemption (5:8-10). They are the overcomers who have their crowns and live in the place prepared for them, where they have gone with Jesus (John 14:1-4).

The twenty-four elders who represent the redeemed in heaven acknowledge that humans were created by God for His good pleasure.

Their response of praise recognizes the sovereignty of God over our lives.

One of the most controversial questions raised by this vision of the throne of God is the identity of the twenty- four elders.

In (Rev. 5:9), the Scriptures tell us the four and twenty elders sang a new song.

Rev. 5:9 "And they sang a new song, saying, thou are worthy to take the book, and to open the seals thereof: for thou were slain, and has redeemed "us" to God by the blood out of every kindred, and tongue, and people, and nation".

Notice "and hast redeemed us", thus revealing their human nature. These twenty-four elders are redeemed men. Once their human nature was confirmed, it became obvious that the Rapture was pictured by (Rev. 4:1), as occurring before the Tribulation. Rapture for this scene, which is of the throne of God in heaven just before the seven-year Tribulation as defined (6-19), pictures twenty-four men or *"elders" in the presence of God.*

There are many significances tied to the number twelve but suffice it to say that God prescribed this number to have meaning and purpose which were governmental authority, completeness or perfection, and the authority given to mankind by God.

Twelve is a spiritual number that has to do with representation. The number twenty-four, I believe, could be two twelves.

(1)   One twelve for the Old Testament.

(2)   One twelve for the New Testament.

The twelve prophets represent the believers of the Old Testament. The twelve disciples represent all believers from the New Testament.

There are many other schools of thought on the twenty-four.

John, "the faithful witness" sees these events at once after the church age has been concluded and just before the beginning of the Tribulation. These men, whether twelve who stand for Israel and twelve who stand for the church, or twenty-four outstanding Christian leaders in all church history, make no difference, they all are redeemed men! They are saved saints who are in heaven just before the revelation of the Tribulation that follows.

Like John, they are part of the pre-tribulation rapture in their glorified bodies, worshiping all three members of the Trinity. This scene in heaven does not occur in the middle of the Tribulation or at its end, but before it begins.

These Old Testament believers were looking forward to Messiah and were preached to when Jesus preached in hell and brought captivity captive out with Him.

Notice all twenty-four were dressed in white robes. White robes are worn by believers in Jesus, who have washed their robes in the blood of Jesus and are made white as snow. All through the Old Testament people like David were looking for the Savior. They believed, even though they were looking forward instead of backward to Him.

There are over thirty-seven Old Testament scriptures that mention the coming of Jesus Christ. These were fulfilled, everyone. It is not absurd to speak of Old Testament believers.

The crowns that they had on their heads were gold. This showed that they had nothing to do with these crowns being put on their heads. Gold means the purity of God. God placed these crowns on their head. The grace of God placed these crowns on their head. They did nothing to earn them. It was a gift from God for believing. Crowns show rulership, and we believers are promised that we will reign with Jesus.

Revelation 4:5 "And out of the throne proceeded lightnings and thundering and voices: and there were seven lamps of fire burning before the throne, which are the seven Spirits of God."

The *"flashes of lightning and thundering"* showed the majesty and awesomeness of God. Lightning, earthquakes, and thundering throughout the Bible have been an outward proclamation of God.

Even at the foot of Mount Sinai, the people were afraid of God because of just such manifestations.

It is not the fury of nature but the firestorm of righteous fury about to come from an awesome, powerful God upon a sinful world (8:5; 11:9; 16:18).

The *"seven lamps"* are a symbolic number covering all the workings of the Spirit of God.

The seven spirits of God refer to the seven eyes of the Lord or characteristics of God (Zech. 4:10 and Isaiah 11:2). "*The seven spirits*" means the entirety of the power of the Spirit is manifest there at the throne and emanates out to the twenty-four or all Christendom. Fire throughout the Bible has been symbolic of God, as in the burning bush (Exodus 3:2). In (Hebrews 12:28-29), we are told to serve God with reverence and Godly fear because God is a consuming fire.

We do not completely understand God, but we must accept and trust God. This burning Spirit of God is to illuminate the minds and Spirits of all who will accept it. Jesus is the Light. Somehow, all three are present in these lamps (Spirit) that illuminate.

Verses 6-8: The *"four beasts" or living creatures, "living ones"*), are probably winged angelic beings (Ezek. 10:15-22), who guard the throne of God. The *"eyes"* symbolize wisdom, and the *"wings" depict movement*. They worship God as did the *seraphim in Isaiah's vision* (Isa. 6:1-3)*. The "lion" stands for strength* (Psalm 103:20), the *"calf" for service* (Heb. 1:14), the *"face" of a "man" intelligence* (Luke 2:52), and the *"eagle" swiftness* (Dan. 9:21). The angelic vision has a strong reference to (Ezekiel 1:4-14).

Revelation 4:6 "And before the throne there was a sea of glass like unto crystal: and amid the throne, and round about the throne, were four beasts full of eyes before and behind."

"A sea of glass": There is no sea in heaven (21:1), but the crystal pavement that serves as the floor of God's throne stretches out like a great, glistening sea (Exodus 24:10; Ezek. 1:22). This *"sea of glass"* reminds me very much of the laver in the tabernacle in the wilderness.

All around the throne were the four beasts. Probably a little better translation would have been living ones. The number "four" shows the universality of these beasts or living beings. In (Isaiah 6:2-13 and Ezekiel 1:5-28), these living beings are also called *"seraphim" and "cherubim"*. These beasts, or living beings, surrounding the throne are full of eyes which means their wisdom was overwhelming.

"Full of eyes": Although not omniscient, an attribute reserved for God alone, these angels have a comprehensive knowledge and belief. Nothing escapes their scrutiny (verse 8).

The eyes denote wisdom or intelligence. These beings looking *"before and behind"* means they look back into times past and look forward to things to come. These living ones, or living beings, also denote *the four gospels, Matthew, Mark, Luke, and John.*

Those books truly are full of wisdom. Matthew does look back at the history of Jesus, and chapter 24 looks ahead to the end times.

Revelation 4:7 "And the first beast was like a lion, and the second beast like a calf, and the third beast had a face as a man, and the fourth beast was like a flying eagle."

*The four living beings show the four gospels: I*n Matthew, Jesus is shown as the Lion of the tribe of Judah. The genealogy of Jesus is in Matthew beginning with verse 1, showing that Jesus truly was the Lion of the tribe of Judah.

"First … like a lion": In what is intended as symbolic language, John compares these 4 beings with 4 of God's earthly creations.

Ezekiel showed that every cherub has these four attributes. The likeness to a lion symbolizes strength and power.

"Second … like a calf": The image of a calf shows that these beings render humble service to God.

"Third … face like that of a man: Their likeness to man shows they are rational beings.

Fourth ... like a flying eagle": The cherubim fulfill their service to God with the swiftness of eagles' wings.

In John 1:1, Jesus, the Word, is God the Word, God the Son. God in the flesh of man. Jesus is the word.

Even though the four gospels tell the same story in essence, they also show four different personalities. You can easily see why these beasts, living beings, are symbolically the four gospels.

Revelation 4:8 "And the four beasts had each of them six wings about him, and they were full of eyes within: and they rest not day and night, saying, Holy, holy, holy, Lord God Almighty, which was, and is, and is to come."

"Full of eyes" (verse 6).

Holy, holy, holy. This is the cry of these heavenly creatures who know God as He is. It has been suggested that each "holy" is directed to one of the members of the Trinity. Then these creatures remind us of the One who "is to come." The return of Christ is guaranteed in the words of these heavenly hosts. In (Acts 1:9-11), angelic beings describe how Christ will return "in like manner as ye have seen him go". Here these angels in heaven reaffirm that promise.

The six wings spoken of (Isaiah 6), seem to show humility, obedience, and reverence to God. The number six makes me believe also, that these wings show work and activity six-day work. It seems here that one of their tasks was to proclaim the holiness of God.

I believe the three *"holy, holy, holy", Lord God Almighty"*, indicate Father, Word, and Holy Ghost. "Which was, and is, and is to come". God's eternal presence is not limited by time, He has always been present and will come.

The *"which was, and is, and is to come"* just furthers that thought and shows us the eternity of these three in one. We do know from (1 John 5), that there are three in heaven.

1 John 5:7 "For there are three that bear record in heaven, the Father, the Word, and the Holy Ghost: and these three are one."

Verses 9-11: All of heaven "*worship*" the Father. The angels extol His character, and the "*elders*" (church), extol His creative powers. God has the right to rule and the sovereign authority to judge the earth, because He is both holy and the Creator of all.

Revelation 4:9 "And when those beasts give glory and honor and thanks to him that sat on the throne, who lives forever and ever,"

It "*when the beasts give glory and honor and thanks*" is a never-ending thing. The four gospels have proclaimed this in the past, are proclaiming it now, and will proclaim it for all of eternity.

"*The giving of "honor"* goes on and on and on. The *giving of "thanks"* is to the Spirit of God, the Trinity.

The song of the living beings is giving praises not just then, not just now, but continuously. We see by this honor given it should be all glory and all honor, etc. The eternity of God is so difficult for us to understand because our minds are programmed to live for just under one hundred years here on earth.

Revelation 4:10 "The four and twenty elders fall before him that sat on the throne, and worship him that live forever and ever, and cast their crowns before the throne, saying,"

In the presence of God, it is a normal thing to fall prostrate at His feet. The "four and twenty elders fall before Him" shows their great humility in the presence of God. A deep respect and honor should be given to God.

"*To Him that sat on the throne*" is very interesting. God the Father is on the central throne, but immediately on His right hand sits God the Son, Jesus. The "throne" encompasses both the Father, the Son, and the Holy Spirit.

The word "*worship*" has been misunderstood by so many. We sing about it in our songs and use it in our prayers. But do we truly know how to worship? Our churches call Sunday services, worship, but again, very little true worship goes on. The word that was translated as "worship" here means "absolute reverence to God, to adore Him".

One of the meanings of the word means to "kiss", like a dog licking his master's hand. Absolute humility and adoration of God is what it means. Do we go to church to humbly worship and adore our God? A deep respect and honor should be given to God.

"Cast their crowns": Aware that God alone handles the rewards they have received, they divest themselves of all honor and cast it at the feet of their King (Rev. 2:10).

Why do they "cast their crowns before the throne"? These crowns are the victorious crowns that Jesus has placed on their head. They, or we, have done nothing to earn the crowns. These crowns belong to Jesus, not us. He won the victory. He placed them on our heads. Everyone benefits from the victory, but Jesus won it. This is another act of humility on their part. When they throw the crowns at Jesus' feet, they are telling Him that they are His because He won them.

Revelation 4:11 "Thou art worthy, O Lord, to receive glory and honor and power: for thou hast created all things, and for thy pleasure they are and were created."

"For thou hast created all things": It is the Creator God who set out to redeem His creation.

We see here the worthiness of God and why He should be praised. It is, in our society, the popular thing to worship the created rather than the Creator. We are warned about this over and over throughout the Bible. Not only in terms of getting our priorities mixed up and thinking too much of money, jewels, family, homes, automobiles, and recreation which can certainly become a God to us, but many are worshipping the sun, moon, stars, and rivers. In far too many Christian homes today we see *totem poles, Buddhas, and all sorts of horoscope paraphernalia.*

God is a jealous God. He will not allow the believer to mess around with false gods. How could we compare the Creator of it all to His creations? We must recognize God to be supreme to all others in every way. Before the world existed, He spoke, and it became. The power of His Word created all that we know.

I believe it is good to understand why He did not just leave well enough alone, live as He was, and not bother with all of this. We have been such a problem and heartache to Him. The earth and all that's on it were created for God's pleasure. He created us so that He could fellowship with us. We are to Jesus like our children are to us. They are great joy, but at the very same time, they can bring us hurt. The joy far outweighs the hurt.

Perhaps that is the way it is with God dealing with us. The joy outweighs the sorrow. We see here that the whole universe was created for God.

Chapter 2

The River of Life

Revelation chapter 22 holds God's Last Message to Humankind. (Rev. 22:6-9), takes us back to the early part of this book, when the faithful and true witness told us that He would send His angel to carry His message concerning the things that must come to pass.

Here at the close of the Bible, we are reintroduced to the Tree of Life, which has not been mentioned in the Bible (Genesis 3), where Adam and Eve sinned in the Garden of Eden. Paradise is restored in the eternal state. All that was lost in the fall is redeemed by the Lamb. The leaves of this tree will be used to heal the relationships of the nations toward each other so that we might live equitably and fairly in eternity.

The picture of eternal life in these verses indicates that we will be busy serving God for all eternity. We will both serve Him (verse 3) and reign with Him (verse 5). Since He is an infinite God, we can be sure He will have infinite things for us to do as we reign there forever. The phrase, "they shall see his face," means that, as believers, we will be granted an audience with the King regularly.

Verses 1-2: These verses depict the abundant life and continuous blessing of the New Jerusalem. One *"river"*, having *"water of life"* (7:17; 21:6; 22:17), comes from God's "throne" and waters the entire city with millennial blessings (Ezek. 47:1-2; Joel 3:18; Zech. 14:8).

The *"tree of life"* pictures eternal sustenance and immortality (verse 14; Gen. 2:9; 3:22). Both the variety and abundance of "fruit" are emphasized. The "healing of the nations" may indicate physical healing during the Millennium (Ezek. 47:12), or the blessings of God in the eternal state.

Revelation 22:1 "And he showed me a pure river of water of life, clear as crystal, proceeding out of the throne of God and the Lamb."

"Pure River of Water of life." In one final glimpse into the future, John sees this river flowing from the throne of God. It is the source of eternal life that emanates from God. Even in heaven, we will drink water and eat food, probably not out of necessity for our health, but because of the pleasure and fellowship it will give us. This is *symbolic of eternal life.*

This river is unlike any on earth because no hydrological cycle exists. *The water of life symbolizes the continual flow of eternal life from God's throne to heaven's inhabitants (Rev.21:6).*

Jesus told the woman at the well if she drank of the water He gave her, she would never thirst again (John 4:14). This is the "water" He was talking about here. This *"water" owned life-giving powers.* The Foundation is the Father and the Lamb. This "water" springs up into everlasting life. In our day of pollution, it is hard to visualize water. When the soldier pierced Jesus' side, water and blood gushed forth (John 19:34). It is the water of life.

Just like everything else in the New Jerusalem, the river was clear as crystal so that it could reflect the glory of God as it cascaded down from the throne of God and of the Lamb in a dazzling, sparkling never. (Revelation 22).

Revelation 22: has God's Last Message to Humankind. (Rev. 22:6-9), takes us back to the early part of this book, when the faithful and true witness told us that He would send His angel to carry His message concerning the things that must come to pass.

Here at the close of the *Bible,* we are reintroduced to *the Tree of Life,* which has not been mentioned in the Bible (Genesis 3), where Adam and Eve sinned in the Garden of Eden.

Paradise is restored in the eternal state. All that was lost in the fall is redeemed by the Lamb.

The leaves of this tree will be used to heal the relationships of the nations toward each other so that we might live equitably and fairly in eternity.

The picture of eternal life in these verses indicates that we will be busy serving God for all eternity.

We will both serve Him (verse 3) and reign with Him (verse 5). Since He is an infinite God, we can be sure He will have infinite things for us to do as we reign there forever. The phrase, *"they shall see his face,"* means that, as believers, we will be granted an audience with the King regularly.

Verses 1-2: These verses depict the abundant life and continuous blessing of the New Jerusalem. One "river", containing "water of life" (7:17; 21:6; 22:17), comes from God's "throne" and waters the entire city millennial blessings (Ezek. 47:1-2; Joel 3:18; Zech. 14:8). *The "tree of life"* pictures eternal sustenance and immortality (compare verse 14; Gen. 2:9; 3:22). Both the variety and abundance of "fruit" are emphasized.

The "*healing of the nations*" may show physical healing during the Millennium (Ezek. 47:12), or the blessings of God in the eternal state.

Revelation 22:1 "And he showed me a pure river of water of life, clear as crystal, proceeding out of the throne of God and the Lamb."

"Pure River of Water of life." In one final glimpse into the future, John sees this river flowing from the throne of God. It is the source of eternal life that emanates from God. Even in heaven, we will drink water and eat food, probably not out of necessity for our health, but because of the pleasure and fellowship it will give us. This is symbolic of eternal life.

This river is unlike any on earth because no hydrological cycle exists. The water of life symbolizes the continual flow of eternal life from God's throne to heaven's inhabitants (21:6).

Jesus told the woman at the well if she drank of the water He gave her, she would never thirst again (John 4:14). This is the "water" He was talking about here. This "water" had life-giving powers.

The Foundation is the father and the Lamb. This "*water*" springs up into everlasting life. In our day of pollution, it is hard to visualize water. When the soldier pierced Jesus' side, water and blood gushed forth (John 19:34). It is the water of life.

Just like everything else in the New Jerusalem, the river was clear as crystal so that it could reflect the glory of God as it cascaded down from the throne of God and of the Lamb in a dazzling, sparkling never-ending flow of everlasting life from God's throne to His people.

Revelation 22:2 "Amid the street of it, and on either side of the river, was there the tree of life, which bare twelve manners of fruits, and yielded her fruit every month: and the leaves of the tree were for the healing of the nations."

A symbol of both eternal life and continual blessing (Gen. 2:9). The tree bears twelve fruits, one for each month, and is symbolic of the abundant variety in heaven. The English word "therapeutic" comes from the Greek word translated "*healing*". The leaves somehow enrich heavenly life, making it full and satisfying.

The Tree of Life was present in the Garden of Eden, but Adam and Eve did not eat of it. It was in the center of the garden Tree of Life – River of Water of Life". I believe this tree is Jesus. When we partake of Him, we have life. The tree bears twelve kinds of fruit that yield its fruit every month suggesting the infinite variety that will fill heaven. This tree offers perpetual life and health as well as food.

Monthly, since time exists no more, emphasizes the expression of the joyous provision of eternity using familiar terms of time.

Nations: meaning the people that are in heaven. Sickness will no longer be, so the healing doesn't imply illness. The leaves therefore will be to promote general health or another way of saying that life in heaven will be fully energized, rich, and exciting continuously.

The scripture also doesn't tell us if we will eat the leaves or the fruit. Angels ate food on earth with Abraham and Sarah as did Jesus after the resurrection with his disciples. Perhaps the saints in heaven will eat for enjoyment and not out of necessity.

"*Verses 3-5:* The effects of the post-Edenic "curse" (Gen. 3:14-19), will be gone forever. God's saints will "serve him" (7:15), and "reign" with Him "forever" (Dan. 7:18, 27).

The greatest blessing of eternity is that "they shall see his face" (Matt. 5:8; Heb. 12:14). Though this is now impossible for an unglorified human being (Exodus 33:20), it will occur in the eternal state. The "*name" of God "in their foreheads*" shows ownership and consecration (3:12; 13:16; Exodus 28:36-38). Since in the New Jerusalem God is always present, His glory makes all other sources of "light" unnecessary (21:23; Isa. 60:19-20; Zech. 14:7).

Revelation 22:3 "And there shall be no more curse: but the throne of God and the Lamb shall be in it; and his servants shall serve him:"

"*There shall be no more curse*": The curse on humanity and the earth because of Adam and Eve's disobedience (Gen. 3:16-19), will be finished. God will never have to judge sin again since it will never exist in the new heaven and new earth.

The one associated with the curse, the old serpent, has been thrown into the lake of fire. The curse of the land is gone. God would not be present here if there was anything cursed left.

The effects of the post-Edenic curse will be gone forever. There will be no more curses. God's saints will serve him (Rev. 7:15), and reign with Him forever (Dan 7:18-27).

The picture of eternal life in these verses indicates that we will be busy serving God for all eternity. We will both serve Him (verse 3), and reign with Him (verse 5). Since He is an infinite God, we can be sure He will have infinite things for us to do as we reign there forever. The phrase, "they shall see his face" means that, as believers, we will be granted an audience with the King regularly.

"His servants shall serve him": This involves the entire revelation which John has just related (Rev. 1:1).

Here we see the "throne of God" and on his right hand is "the Lamb". These "servants" that shall serve him are us. We Christians have been bought and paid for with the blood of the Lamb. We will be with the Lamb and the Father but we will not be their equal. We will be their servants.

Revelation 22:4 "And they shall see his face; and his name shall be in their foreheads."

"See his face": No unglorified human could see God's face and live (Exodus 33:20-23). But the residents of heaven can look on God's face without harm because they are now holy (John 1:18; 1 Tim. 6:16; 1 John 3:2).

The greatest blessing of eternity is that they shall see his face (Matt. 5:8; Heb. 12:14). Though this is now impossible for an unglorified human being (Exodus 33:20), it will occur in the eternal state. The name of God in their foreheads shows ownership and consecration (Rev. 3:12; 13:16; Exodus 28:36-38).

Throughout the Bible, we have been taught that you cannot look upon the face of God and live. Even Moses, who was so close to God, wanted to see God, and God told him no. He put His hand over Moses and passed by him, and Moses saw his backside (Exodus 33:22). There we will be in his presence all the time and can look in his face anytime we want to. We are sealed with the Lamb's seal.

The saints in New Jerusalem will see God's face. Being perfectly holy and righteous, they'll be able to endure the blazing, glorious light from God's presence without being consumed. That was impossible for mortal men.

Revelation 22:5 "And there shall be no night there, and they need no candle, neither light of the sun; for the Lord God giveth them light: and they shall reign forever and ever."

Since in the New Jerusalem God is always present, His glory makes all other sources of light unnecessary (Rev. 21:23; Isaiah 60:19-20; Zech. 14:7).

We have talked so much about our Lord Jesus being the Light. He is the source of all Light. When the Light is on full power, you certainly do not need a candle. The sun has no more purpose anymore either. The presence of this Light is all they need. This Kingdom has no end. It is for all of eternity.

"They shall reign": Heaven's citizens are more than servants (3:21).

As a final word describing the saint's heavenly experience, they are told once again that it will never end. They shall reign forever and forever.

(Verses 6 to 9), takes us back to the early part of this book, when the faithful and true witness told us that He would send His angel to convey His message concerning the things that must come to pass. Christ speaks the sixth blessing (beatitude), to those who treat the prophesies of this book as "faithful and true", and then live accordingly.

Revelation 22:6 "And he said unto me, these sayings are faithful and true: and the Lord God of the holy prophets sent his angel to show unto his servants the things which must shortly be done."

"His servants": The members of the seven churches of Asia Minor who received this letter (1:11), and then all believers who have read, or will read it since.

"The things which must shortly be done: This involves the entire revelation which John has just related (John 1:1).

(Verses 6-21), form a conclusion or summary of the book. They emphasize two themes:

(1) The genuineness of the book as a revelation from God; and

(2) The nearness of the return of Christ.

These sayings refer to the entire Book of Revelation. They are authenticated as genuine by the angel whom God sent to give them through John to His servants. That is the members of the churches (Rev. 1:3, 11).

Here is just a reassurance that all of this is not to be taken lightly. This is the absolute truth. The prophets such as Daniel, Ezekiel, and Isaiah (to name just a few), have all spoken of this special time in history. We even read this (Matthew 24; Luke 21 and 22).

The angel's words reinforce an important truth: Everything John saw in Revelation will come to pass. John's words are not mystical, and the Apocalypse is not a record of his bizarre dreams or the result of an overactive imagination. Further, it is not an allegory a form of translation, from which readers can find hidden meanings of their concoction. It is an accurate description of events and persons that are yet to come.

Revelation 22:7 "Behold, I come quickly: blessed is he that keep the sayings of the prophecy of this book."

This is Jesus speaking when He says, *"Behold, I come quickly"*. Jesus' return is imminent (3:11).

"Blessed is he that keeps the saying of the prophecy of this book" (Rev. 1:3). This is referring to the reading of the Book of Revelation. But how in the world can you keep the sayings, if you don't know what these sayings are? Most people avoid Revelation like the plague, but if we must keep the sayings, then we must read and understand what they are. I believe this book also means the entire Bible.

Believers are called to guard or protect the book of Revelation. To defend against detractors who deny its relevance, against those critics who deny its veracity and authority as well as against confused interpreters who obscure its meaning. They are called to not only guard Scripture but also to obey it.

You might ask, what does it mean to obey the book of Revelation? Think of it as a general command to long for Christ's return and our eternal fellowship with Him. It calls believers to want heaven, to wish holiness, to want to see Christ vindicated, and for Him to triumph over His enemies. To desire the end of the curse and to desire the glories of

Christ's earthly kingdom and the new heaven and the new earth (New Heaven and the New Earth").

To see God's face, to see an end to the Babylonian Harlot and the corrupt commercial and political system, and to look forward to a life of peace and happiness.

Thus, the purpose of Revelation is not to provide entertainment and to merely satisfy the curiosity of believers about the future, but to reveal the glory of God's Son and call believers to live godly, obedient lives considering His soon return.

Verses 8-11: "John" certifies that he has seen and "heard" everything that he has written in the book. He again makes the mistake of worshiping the messenger ("angel"), of God rather than "God" Himself (19:10). Angels are simply "fellow servants" of God (Psalm 103:20; Dan. 7:10; Heb. 1:14). In contrast with Daniel, who was told to *"seal" up* his book of prophecy (since the end was still in the distant future (compare Dan. 12:4, 9, 13), John is told to leave his book open ("Seal not"). The Messiah has come, His return is imminent, and thus "the time is at hand". Verse 11 is not a command, but rather a statement of fact and a warning. Character tends to become fixed and unchangeable, decided by a lifetime of habitual action.

The arrival of the end will prevent any change of destiny. When Christ returns, the deliberate choice of each person will have fixed his eternal fate.

Revelation 22:8 "And I John saw these things and heard them. And when I had heard and seen, I fell to worship before the feet of the angel which showed me these things."

"Heard and seen": John resumes speaking for the first time since Chapter 1 and confirms the veracity of the revelation with his eyewitness testimony, the basis of any reliable witness.

Several times in Revelation, we see John overwhelmed by the presence and the power this angel shows him. He, being overcome by the magnitude of it all, starts to worship this angel. Some people have false doctrines centered on angel worship. We must not worship angels. They are created beings. We must worship the Creator. We are warned over and over not to worship angels. John is told several times in Revelation not to worship this angel (19:10).

Revelation 22:9 "Then saith he unto me, see thou do it not: for I am thy fellow servant, and of thy brethren the prophets, and of them which keep the sayings of this book: worship God."

The angel quickly reminds the apostle that he too, was a created being by his declaration. Not only his, but also of John's brethren the prophets, and of all believers that are defined here as *"Them which keep the sayings of this book."*

Then the angel commands John to worship God as God alone is the only acceptable Person to worship. The Bible forbids the worship of anyone else including angels, saints, the Virgin Mary, or any other created being.

Revelation 22:10 "And he saith unto me, Seal not the sayings of the prophecy of this book: for the time is at hand."

"Seal not the sayings of the prophecy" (10:11). Previous prophecies were sealed up (Dan. 8:26; 12:4-10). These prophecies are to be proclaimed so they can produce obedience and worship.

The command not to seal this prophetic message is quite different than what the Lord told Daniel.

Dan 12:4 "But thou, O Daniel, shut up the words, and seal the book, even to the time of the end".

"The time is at hand": This refers to forthcomingness, which means that the end is next.

The reason for the difference in the instructions is simply said, "The time is at hand." Until the death and resurrection of Christ, the time for this prophecy had not come. Since Jesus already opened the seven seals prophetically (Rev.: 5 and 6), to reveal the future, it is only appropriate that the entire book remain open for us to read as well.

In contrast with Daniel, who was told to "seal" up his book of prophecy since the end was still in the distant future, here John is told to leave his book open and Seal not. The Messiah had come, His second coming is imminent, and thus now the time is at hand.

The reason for the difference in the instructions is that one lived after the time of Christ's crucifixion, the other before. On John's Day, it was possible to see the unfolding of the events prophesied; on Daniel's Day, they were a long way off. ending the flow of everlasting life from God's throne to His people.

Revelation 22:2 "Amid the street of it, and on either side of the river, was there the tree of life, which bare twelve manners of fruits, and yielded her fruit every month: and the leaves of the tree were for the healing of the nations."

A symbol of both eternal life and continual blessing (Gen. 2:9). The tree bears twelve fruits, one for each month, and is symbolic of the abundant variety in heaven. The English word "*therapeutic*" comes from the Greek word translated "*healing*". The leaves somehow enrich heavenly life, making it full and satisfying.

The Tree of Life was present in the Garden of Eden, but Adam and Eve did not eat of it. It was in the center of the garden *Tree of Life – River of Water of Life*". I believe this tree is Jesus.

When we partake of Him, we have life. The tree bears twelve kinds of fruit that yield its fruit every month suggesting the infinite variety that will fill heaven. This tree offers perpetual life and health as well as food.

Monthly, since time exists no more, emphasizes the expression of the joyous provision of eternity using familiar terms of time.

Nations: meaning the people that are in heaven. Sickness will no longer be, so the healing doesn't imply illness. The leaves therefore will be to promote general health or another way of saying that life in heaven will be fully energized, rich, and exciting continuously.

The scripture also doesn't tell us if we will eat the leaves or the fruit. Angels ate food on earth with Abraham and Sarah as did Jesus after the resurrection with his disciples. Perhaps the saints in heaven will eat for enjoyment and not out of necessity.

"Verses 3-5: The effects of the post-Edenic "curse" (Gen. 3:14-19), will be gone forever. God's saints will *"serve him"* (7:15), and *"reign"* with Him "forever" (Dan. 7:18, 27). The greatest blessing of eternity is that "they shall see his face" (Matt. 5:8; Heb. 12:14). Though this is now impossible for an unglorified human being (compare Exodus 33:20), it will occur in the eternal state. The "name" of God *"in their foreheads"* shows ownership and consecration (Rev. 3:12; 13:16; Exodus 28:36-38).

Since in the New Jerusalem God is always present, His glory makes all other sources of "light" unnecessary (Rev. 21:23; Isa. 60:19-20; Zech. 14:7).

Revelation 22:3 "And there shall be no more curse: but the throne of God and the Lamb shall be in it; and his servants shall serve him:"

"There shall be no more curse": The curse on humanity and the earth because of Adam and Eve's disobedience (Gen. 3:16-19), will be finished. God will never have to judge sin again since it will never exist in the new heaven and new earth.

The one associated with the curse, the old serpent, has been thrown into the lake of fire. The curse of the land is gone. God would not be present here if there was anything cursed left.

The effects of the post-Edenic curse will be gone forever. There will be no more curses. God's saints will serve him (Rev. 7:15), and reign with Him forever (Dan 7:18-27).

The picture of eternal life in these verses indicates that we will be busy serving God for all eternity. We will both serve Him (verse 3), and reign with Him (verse 5). Since He is an infinite God, we can be sure He will have infinite things for us to do as we reign there forever. The phrase, *"they shall see his face"* means that, as believers, we will be granted an audience with the King regularly.

"His servants shall serve him": This involves the entire revelation which John has just related (Rev1:1).

Here we see the *"throne of God"* and on his right hand is *"the Lamb".* These "servants" that shall serve him are us. We Christians have been bought and paid for with the blood of the Lamb. We will be with the Lamb and the Father, but we will not be their equal. We will be their servants.

Revelation 22:4 "And they shall see his face; and his name shall be in their foreheads."

"See his face": No unglorified human could see God's face and live (Exodus 33:20-23). But the residents of heaven can look on God's face without harm because they are now holy (John 1:18; 1 Tim. 6:16; 1 John 3:2).

The greatest blessing of eternity is that they shall see his face (Matt. 5:8; Heb. 12:14). Though this is now impossible for an unglorified human being (Exodus 33:20), it will occur in the eternal state. The name of God in their foreheads shows ownership and consecration (Rev. 3:12; 13:16; Exodus 28:36-38).

Throughout the Bible, we have been taught that you cannot look upon the face of God and live. Even Moses, who was so close to God, wanted to see God, and God told him no. He put His hand over Moses and passed by him, and Moses saw his backside (Exodus 33:22). There we will be in his presence all the time and can look in his face anytime we want to. We are sealed with the Lamb's seal.

The saints in New Jerusalem will see God's face. Being perfectly holy and righteous, they'll be able to endure the blazing, glorious light from God's presence without being consumed. That was impossible for mortal men.

Revelation 22:5 "And there shall be no night there; they need no candle, neither light of the sun; for the Lord God giveth them light: and they shall reign forever and ever."

Since in the New Jerusalem God is always present, His glory makes all other sources of light unnecessary (Rev. 21:23; Isaiah 60:19-20; Zech. 14:7).

We have talked so much about our Lord Jesus being the Light. He is the foundation of all Light. When the Light is on full power, you certainly do not need a candle. The sun has no more purpose anymore either. The presence of this Light is all they need. This Kingdom has no end. It is for all of eternity.

"They shall reign": Heaven's citizens are more than servants (3:21).

As a final word describing the saint's heavenly experience, they are told it once again that it will never end. They shall reign forever and forever.

(Verses 6 to 9), takes us back to the early part of this book, when the faithful and true witness told us that He would send His angel to carry His message concerning the things that must come to pass. Christ speaks the sixth blessing (beatitude), to those who treat the prophesies of this book as "_faithful and true",_ and then live accordingly.

Revelation 22:6 "And he said unto me, these sayings are faithful and true: and the Lord God of the holy prophets sent his angel to show unto his servants the things which must shortly be done."

"His servants": The members of the seven churches of Asia Minor who received this letter (1:11), and then all believers who have read, or will read it since.

"The things which must shortly be done: This involves the entire revelation which John has just related (1:1).

(Verses 6-21), form a conclusion or summary of the book. They emphasize two themes:

(1) The truth of the book as a revelation from God

(2) The nearness of the return of Christ.

These sayings refer to the entire Book of Revelation. They are true as sincere by the angel whom God sent to give them through John to His servants. That is the members of the churches (Rev. 1:3, 11).

Here is just a reassurance that all of this is not to be taken lightly. This is the absolute truth. The prophets such as Daniel, Ezekiel, and Isaiah to name just a few, have all spoken of this distinct time in history. We even read this (Matthew 24; Luke 21 and 22). It is the same information, regardless of who pens it, because the author is God.

The angel's words reinforce an important truth: Everything John saw in Revelation will come to pass. John's words are not mystical, and the Apocalypse is not a record of his bizarre dreams or the result of an overactive mind. Further, it is not a metaphor a form of translation, from which readers can find hidden meanings of their concoction. It is an accurate description of events and persons that are yet to come.

Revelation 22:7 "Behold, I come quickly: blessed is he that keep the sayings of the prophecy of this book."

This is Jesus speaking when He says, "*Behold, I come quickly*". Jesus' return is imminent (3:11).

"Blessed is he that keeps the saying of the prophecy of this book" (Rev. 1:3). This is referring to the reading of the Book of Revelation. But how in the world can you keep the sayings, if you don't know what these sayings are? Most people avoid Revelation like the plague, but if we must keep the sayings, then we must read and understand what they are. I believe this book covers the entire Bible.

Believers are called to guard or protect the book of Revelation. To defend against detractors who deny its significance, against those critics who deny its veracity and authority as well as against confused interpreters who obscure its meaning. They are called to not only guard Scripture but also to obey it.

You might ask, what does it mean to obey the book of Revelation? Think of it as a general command to long for Christ's return and our eternal fellowship with Him. It calls believers to want heaven, to wish holiness, to desire to see Christ vindicated, and for Him to triumph over His enemies. To desire the end of the curse and to desire the glories of Christ's earthly kingdom and the new heaven and the new earth.

To see God's face, to see an end to *the Babylonian Harlot and the corrupt commercial and political system,* to look forward to a life of peace and happiness.

Thus, the purpose of Revelation is not to provide entertainment and to merely satisfy the curiosity of believers about the future, but to reveal the glory of God's Son and call believers to live godly, obedient lives considering His soon return.

Verses 8-11: "John" certifies that he has seen and "heard" everything that he has written in the book. He again makes the mistake of worshiping the messenger ("*angel*"), of God rather than "God" Himself (Rev.19:10). Angels are simply "fellow servants" of God (Psalm 103:20; Dan. 7:10; Heb. 1:14). In contrast with Daniel, who was told to *"seal" up his book of prophecy* since the end was still in the distant future (Dan. 12:4, 9, 13), John is told to leave his book open *("Seal not").* The Messiah has come, His return is impending, and thus "the time is at hand". Verse 11 is not a command, but rather a statement of fact and a warning. Character tends to become fixed and unchangeable, determined by a lifetime of habitual action. The arrival of the end will prevent any change of destiny. When Christ returns, the deliberate choice of each person will have fixed his eternal fate.

Revelation 22:8 "And I John saw these things and heard them. And when I had heard and seen, I fell to worship before the feet of the angel which showed me these things."

"Heard and seen": John resumes speaking for the first time since Chapter 1 and confirms the veracity of the revelation with his eyewitness testimony, the basis of any reliable witness.

Several times in Revelation, we see John overwhelmed by the presence and the power this angel shows him. He, being overcome by the greatness of it all, starts to worship this angel. Some people have false doctrines centered on angel worship. We must not worship angels. They are created beings. We must worship the Creator. We are warned over and over not to worship angels. John is told several times in Revelation not to worship this angel (Rev. 19:10).

Revelation 22:9 "Then saith he unto me, see thou do it not: for I am thy fellow servant, and of thy brethren the prophets, and of them which keep the sayings of this book: worship God."

The angel quickly reminds the apostle that he too, was a created being by his declaration. Not only his, but also of John's brethren the prophets, and of all believers that are defined here as "Them which keep the sayings of this book."

Then the angel commands John to worship God as God alone is the only acceptable Person to worship. The Bible forbids the worship of anyone else including angels, saints, the Virgin Mary, or any other created being.

Revelation 22:10 "And he saith unto me, Seal not the sayings of the prophecy of this book: for the time is at hand."

"Seal not the sayings of the prophecy" (Rev.10:11). Previous prophecies were sealed up (Dan. 8:26; 12:4-10). These prophecies are to be proclaimed so they can produce obedience and worship.

The command not to seal this prophetic message is quite different than what the Lord told Daniel.

Dan 12:4 "But thou, O Daniel, shut up the words, and seal the book, even to the time of the end".

"The time is at hand": This refers to imminency, which means that the end is next.

The reason for the difference in the instructions is simply stated, "the time is at hand." Until the death and resurrection of Christ, the time for this prophecy had not come. Since Jesus already opened the seven seals prophetically (Rev.: 5 and 6), to reveal the future, it is only appropriate that the entire book remain open for us to read as well.

In contrast with Daniel, who was told to *"seal"* up his book of prophecy since the end was still in the distant future, here John is told to leave his book open (_Seal up what the angel spoke._). The Messiah had come, His second coming is forthcoming, and thus now the time is at hand.

The reason for the difference in the instructions is that one lived after the time of Christ's crucifixion, the other before. On John's Day, it was possible to see the unfolding of the events prophesied; on Daniel's Day, they were a long way off.

Revelation 22:11 "He that is unjust, let him be unjust still: and he which is filthy, let him be filthy still: and he that is righteous, let him be righteous still: and he that is holy, let him be holy still."

Those who reject God's warnings will fix their eternal destiny in hell, where they will retain their evil and filthy natures for all eternity. Those who respond to the warnings will fix their eternal destiny in glory and realize perfect righteousness and holiness in heaven.

Verse 11 is not a command, but rather a statement of fact and a warning. Character tends to become fixed and unchangeable, determined by a lifetime of habitual action. The arrival of the end will prevent any change of destiny.

Those who hear the truth but continue to do wrong, will by that hardened response fix their eternal destiny in hell. Conversely, those who continue to practice righteousness and keep themselves holy give evidence of genuine saving faith.

When Christ returns, the deliberate choice of each person will have fixed his eternal fate.

We cannot cover up from God. God sees into the heart. If you are a sinner, He already knows it. You do not have to tell Him. If you belong to Jesus, He knows that too. Whatever you are down deep, Jesus already knows.

Verses 12-13: Again, Christ declares the imminence of His return. "_Reward_" is always based on "_work_" (Jer. 17:10; Rom. 2:6; 1 Peter 1:17). For believers, there is the judgment seat of Christ (2 Cor. 5:10; Dan. 12:2 for Old Testament saints). For unbelievers, there are various judgments, culminating in the Great White Throne judgment (20:11-15; Matt. 25:31-46).

The three designations (of verse 13) are virtually equivalent in meaning. By applying them to Himself, Christ claims unlimited, eternal equality with God (1:8, 17; 2:8; 21:6).

Revelation 22:12 "And, behold, I come quickly; and my reward is with me, to give every man according as his work shall be."

"I come quickly" (3:11). Again, imminence is the issue (compare Mark 13:33-37).

Again, Christ declares the imminence of His return. This is in red in the Bible, so this is Jesus speaking directly here. All Christians should be watching the eastern sky for "In a moment when you think not, the eastern sky will open, the trumpet will blow, and Jesus shall shout". At that time, we will be called to heaven to be with Him forever ("Rapture").

"According as his work shall be: Only those works which survive God's testing fire have eternal value and are worthy of reward (1 Cor. 3:10-15; 4:1-5; 2 Cor. 5:10).

Our rewards will be for the things *(treasures),* we have stored in heaven. Rewards are always based on works done by believers based on their faithfulness in serving Christ in this life ("*Rewards in Heaven for Christians*"). Their works will be tested and only those with eternal value "will be revealed by fire, and the fire shall try every man's work of what sort it is" (1 Cor. 3:13).

The rewards believers will enjoy in heaven will be abilities for serving God. The greater their faithfulness is in this life, the greater will be their opportunity to serve in heaven, not to mention the crowns believers will receive.

Knowing that Jesus could return at any moment shouldn't lead Christians to a life of idle waiting for His coming. Instead, it should produce diligent, obedient, worshipful service to God and urgent proclamation of the gospel to unbelievers.

Try looking at it this way. By telling everyone you meet now about the good news of Jesus, but they don't listen to you, then suddenly the Rapture happens, and those people will then remember every word you said to them. That is why I believe that right after the Rapture, more people will begin immediately to seek the truth about Jesus and that will begin the largest soul harvest the world has ever known.

Revelation 22:13 "I am Alpha and Omega, the beginning and the end, the first and the last."

"I am Alpha and Omega" (1:8).

The three designations of verse 13 are virtually equivalent in meaning.

(1) *Alpha and Omega.*

(2) *The beginning and the end.*

(3) *The first and the last.*

By applying them to Himself, Christ claims unlimited, eternal equality with God (Rev. 1:8, 17; 2:8; 21:6).

These three designations express Christ's infinity, eternity, and boundless life transcending all limitations. These descriptions describe the completeness, timelessness, and sovereign authority of the Lord Jesus Christ.

Verses 14-15: "They that do his commandments" are believers (12:17; 14:12; Matt. 7:13-21; 1 John 3:10). The "tree of life" indicates immortality and divine blessing (2:7; 22:2). To be able to "enter in through the gates into the city" is to have heavenly citizenship in the eternal dwelling place of God and redeemed mankind. All unbelievers are "without" (outside), the city (i.e., in the lake of fire; (verse 15; 21:8, 27).

The *"dogs" are impure and malicious people* (Deut. 23:17-18; Phil. 3:2). *"Sorcerers" are those who practice witchcraft* (Greek Pharmakos). *"Whoremongers" are those who practice all kinds of sexual immorality* (Greek pornos; 1 Cor. 6:9-10). "Lie" (see 12:9; Prov. 6:16-19; 12:22; l John 8:44).

Revelation 22:14 "Blessed are they that do his commandments, that they may have right to the tree of life and may enter in through the gates into the city. "

"Blessed are they that do his commandments" (1:3). This symbolizes those who have been forgiven of their sins, who have been cleansed by the blood of the Lamb of God (Heb. 9:14; 1 Peter 1:18-19; see note on 7:14).

The Bible makes it clear that salvation is a matter of the will, whosoever wishes may come. This implies that *whosoever will "not" come is lost.* This teaching abounds throughout the Scriptures. In contrast to those who reject Christ, we encounter the state of the blessed described here (verse 14). Those who have washed their robes in the righteousness of Christ have a right to the Tree of Life and thus are entitled to live forever.

He describes their state as "blessed," meaning "happy". Every individual wants happiness. The way to eternal happiness is to receive Christ as Lord and Savior, which entitles you to entrance into the Holy City, access to the Tree of Life, and the marvelous blessings of a loving God. If there is any question in your mind as to whether you have received the living Christ, I urge you, based on His challenge, to change your will and receive Him as your Lord and Savior today.

They who do his commandments are believers.

John 14:15: "If ye love me, keep my commandments". (Rev. 12:17; 14:12; Matt. 7:13- 21; 1 John 3:6-10).

"Tree of life" (2; Gen. 2:9).

The Tree of Life shows immortality and divine blessing (Rev. 2:7; 22:2). To be able to enter through the gates into the city is to have heavenly citizenship in the eternal dwelling place of God and redeemed mankind *("Tree of Life – River of Water of Life").*

All unbelievers are without outside the city, i.e., in the lake of fire (Rev. 21:8), for a list of the type of sins that exclude people from heaven that was given to John. Also (Rev. 21:27).

James 1:22" But be ye doers of the word, and not hearers only, deceiving yourselves."

You see, we are to be about the father's business. If we truly are sold out to God and have made Jesus the Lord of our lives, our hearts will desire to do His Commandments. The Jews were the natural branches of the tree. We Christians when we are born again, are grafted into the Tree of Life, who is Jesus Christ our Lord.

Revelation 22:15 "For without are dogs, and sorcerers, and whoremongers, and murderers, and idolaters, and whosoever loveth and maketh a lie."

"Dogs": Considered wicked and unclean beings in New Testament times. The term when applied to people referred to anyone of low moral character. Unfaithful leaders (Isa. 56:10), and homosexual prostitutes (Deut. 23:18; Lev 18.22), are among those who received such a designation.

Sorcerers are those who practice the occult or witchcraft. Greek "Pharmakos" is the root of the English word pharmacy which often accompanies those practices (9:21).

Whoremongers: are those who practice all kinds of sexual immorality. Greek "pornos" is the root of the English word pornography.

Murderers: means pre-meditated murder. This has nothing to do with accidental killing or killing in war. (Rev. 21:8).

Rev. 21:8 "But the fearful, and unbelieving, and the abominable, and murderers, and whoremongers, and sorcerers, and idolaters, and all liars, shall have their part in the lake which burn with fire and brimstone: which is the second death."

Idolaters are just those who put anything ahead of God which includes mammon (money), family, or the love of everything which takes one's attention off serving God. Someone once said: Show me someone's calendar and checkbook and I'll tell you where their heart lies. Think about that. Idolaters are also those who worship false gods or unacceptably worship the true God.

Make at Lie: Everyone sometimes during their life has lied as It's human nature. Some tell little white lies, even some Christians. But all lies are acts of deception and can be very harmful to others. Simply withholding some of the truth when asked a question is lying. A lie does not care who tells it.

Consider carefully how you answer and instead of a white lie or withholding a part of the truth, find another way. I would rather be told the truth no matter how bad it is than find later I had been deceived. Those who "love and make a lie" have to do with hurting someone else. Any time we hurt someone else, it is a sin.

Not all who have ever committed any of these sins listed above will be excluded from heaven. But it is those who love and habitually practice these sins and stubbornly cling to them and refuse Christ's invitation to salvation who will be the ones cast into the lake of fire.

Verses 16-17: "Jesus" now authenticates His "angel" through whom He has given this revelation to John (1:1). "You" is plural, showing that the revelation is for all the churches.

As "the root and the offspring of David", Jesus is the fulfillment of the messianic promise of (Isaiah 11:1; 5:5; Rom. 1:3). As "the bright and Morningstar", Jesus will shortly bring in the new age: the messianic kingdom (Num. 24:17; Rom. 13:11-12; 2 Peter 1:19).

Revelation 22:16 "I Jesus have sent mine angel to testify unto you these things in the churches. I am the root and the offspring of David, and the bright and morning star."

"I Jesus have sent mine angel to testify." This is the first time that the words "I Jesus", appear in the bible. It establishes that this final invitation in Scripture is not a human invitation, but a divine call issued personally to sinners by the Lord Jesus Christ Himself (1:1).

"The churches": The seven churches of Asia Minor who were the book's original recipients (1:11).

This verse is Jesus' seal of approval on the whole book of Revelation. It marks the first use of the word "church" since chapter three. Why is there no reference to the Church during the time of tribulation on earth described in chapters 6 through 18? Because the church, having been raptured to heaven, will not be on earth.

"*The root and the offspring of David*": Christ is the source ("root"), of David's life and line of descendants, which set up His deity. He is also a "descendant" of David, which establishes His humanity. This phrase gives powerful testimony to Christ as the Godman (2 Tim. 2:8).

How can Jesus be "the root and the offspring of David" both? In the Flesh this is impossible. David, in the flesh, was the ancestor of Jesus. In the Spirit, Jesus was David's ancestor. Jesus was David's God.

We read (2 Peter):

2 Peter 1:19 "We have also a surer word of prophecy; whereunto ye do well that ye take heed, as unto a light that shineth in a dark place, until the day dawn, and the day star arise in your hearts:"

"*Bright and morning star*": This is the brightest star announcing the arrival of the day. When Jesus comes, He will be the brightest star who will shatter the darkness of man's night and herald the dawn of God's glorious day (2:28).

You see, it is not unusual in a symbolic way to speak of Jesus as a star. Here is our Bright Star. Until we receive this Star into our life, we are full of darkness.

Verse 17 has four invitations to the unsaved to "come" to Christ in faith for eternal life. The *"Spirit" is the Holy Spirit, and the "bride" is the church* (19:7-9; 21:9). The Holy Spirit works through the church to evangelize the world. The "water of life" is eternal life, available "freely" by faith in Christ (7:17, 21:6; Isa. 55:1; John 4:14; 7:37).

Revelation 22:17 "And the Spirit and the bride say, Come. And let him that heareth say, Come. And let him that is athirst come. And whosoever will, let him take the water of life freely."

"*Come*": This is the Spirit's and church's answer to the promise of His coming.

The Holy Spirit, since the beginning, has been saying "Come". Unless the Holy Spirit of God woos you, you can forget being saved. It is God's wish that all should be saved. I believe what this is saying, in this instance, is that the Spirit and the believers are saying, "Come quickly Lord Jesus". Salvation is open to whosoever will.

"*Let him that hearsay*": This is an unlimited offer of grace and salvation to all who want to have their thirsty souls quenched (Isa. 55:1-2).

The Lord's Last Invitation to Humankind. The Lord Jesus Christ, ever concerned for the souls of the lost, closes His great revelation with a challenge for individual people to call on His name. He shows that there are two who invites us to come to Him: the "Spirit" and the "bride". In addition, He will even use "him who hears."

God the Holy Spirit will use the printed page as well as those who are just repeating what they have heard but may not even believe what they are saying. He also uses the "bride", which shows that the primary ministry of the Church of Christ during the entire Church Age is to tell others about the Savior.

All Christians everywhere should be engaged in saying to their fellow human beings: "Whoever is thirsty, let him come; and whoever wishes, let him take the gift of the water of life." Jesus Christ, of course, is the water of life ("Christian – How Do I Become a Christian?").

Everyone has a hunger and thirst for God. Some do not know what they are hungering for. It is so simple just to give in and let Jesus bring you salvation, peace, joy, and life that lasts forever. When we take of this Water of Jesus, it brings Eternal Life (verse 1). The water, Spirit, and blood testify for us and assure us of a heavenly home (John 5:8).

Verses 18-19: Jesus offers extended testimony on the authority and finality of the prophecy. He commissioned John to write it, but He was its author. These are not the first such warnings (Deut. 4:2; 12:32; Prov. 30:6; Jer. 26:2). These warnings against altering the biblical text represent the close of the New Testament canon. Anyone who tampers with the truth by attempting to falsify, mitigate, alter, or misinterpret it will incur the judgments described in these verses.

The speaker is Christ Himself (verse 20), who thus claims canonicity for the book and the entire New Testament equal to that of the Old Testament. Anyone who willfully distorts the message of the Book of Revelation shows himself not to be a genuine believer and will not participate in eternal life or the blessings of the New Jerusalem. Almost all Greek manuscripts read *"Tree of Life" instead of "Book of Life".*

Revelation 22:18 "For I testify unto every man that heareth the words of the prophecy of this book, if any man shall add unto these things, God shall add unto him the plagues that are written in this book:"

The speaker who testifies to the authority and finality of the words of the prophecy of this book is the Lord Jesus Christ.

A severe warning to the detractors from this prophecy. I (Jesus) warn everyone who hears the words of the prophecy of this book: If anyone adds anything to them, God will add to him the plagues described in this book.

And if anyone takes words away from this book of prophecy, God will take away from him his share in the Tree of Life and in the holy city, which is described in this book.

Revelation 22:19 "And if any man shall take away from the words of the book of this prophecy, God shall take away his part out of the book of life, and out of the holy city, and from the things which are written in this book."

This is one of the most awesome challenges in the Word of God against tampering with Holy Writing. Far too many today glibly ridicule, detract from, and cast disparaging remarks on Holy Scripture. This is their day of opportunity, but their judgment will come upon them swiftly in God's good time. It is a fearful thing to disbelieve God, and it is unbelief that causes someone to detract from His Holy Word.

Although this is not a reference to Bible-believing commentators of the Word who mistakenly translate some passage and inadvertently minimize it. The Lord's warning here is addressed to those who engage in deliberate falsification or misinterpretation of Scripture, those whom Paul denounces as corruptors of the Word of God (2 Cor. 2:17).

Still, it does serve as a soul-stirring challenge to those who have taken in hand to write and preach on this marvelous book.

Verses 20-21: The final promise of Christ in the Bible is that His return is imminent (see also verses 7, 12). *"Amen"* means *"truly" or "so be it".* The believer's response is simply, "Come, Lord Jesus", which is the equivalent of the Aramaic *"Maranatha"* (1 Cor. 16:22).

The answer to the problems of life is to be found in the return of the sovereign Son of God. Verse 21 is a benediction of "grace" (Rom. 16:24; 1 Cor. 16:23; Phil. 4:23; 1 Thess. 5:28; 2 Thess. 3:18; Mal. 4:6d).

Revelation 22:20 "He which testified these things saith, Surely, I come quickly. Amen. Even so, come, Lord Jesus."

"Surely I come quickly" (3:11). Considering this future expectation, what is now required of believers is outlined by Peter (2 Peter 3:11-18).

As previously said, the translation is *"Surely I come suddenly"*, when least expected. The cry of every Christian should be *"Come quickly Lord Jesus"*, as I said before. My cry, as I go through the land telling people of my Savior and Lord, is *"JESUS IS COMING".*

John speaks for all true believers when he writes, *"Come Lord Jesus"*, since Christians are those "who have loved His appearing" (2 Tim. 4:8). Scoffers may mockingly ask, *"Where is the promise of His coming?* For ever since the fathers fell asleep, all continues just as it was from the beginning of creation" (2 Peter 3:4). But things will not continue forever as they are. Jesus will return, just as Revelation predicts. If the certainty of Christ's return to judge sinners does not motivate people to repent, then nothing will.

"Amen" means so be it.

Revelation 22:21 "The grace of our Lord Jesus Christ be with you all. Amen

This scripture is an expression of God's grace toward fallen humanity.

Without the *"grace of our Lord Jesus*," none of us would be saved. While we were yet in sin, Jesus died for us. Salvation is a gift of God.

The letters of *GRACE* are commonly known as God's Riches at Christ's Expense.

The Lord of Glory, as He promised in Scripture, offers heaven exclusively to those who accept His gracious invitation. Without the "grace of us.

Chapter 3

The Eight Beatitudes of Jesus

Verses 1-2: The opening verses of the Sermon on the Mount indicate that this message deals with the inner state of mind and heart that is the indispensable absolute of true Christian discipleship. It delineates the outward manifestations of character and conduct of true believers and genuine disciples.

Thus, the believer's life, described by Jesus in the Sermon on the Mount, is a life of grace and glory from God alone.

To make this quality of life the product of man's human efforts, as does the generous, is the height of overestimating man's ability and underestimating his depravity.

To relegate this entire message, Jesus' longest recorded sermon, to a Jewish-only lifestyle, as do some dispensationalists, is to rob the church of her most significant statement of faithful Christian living.

The Sermon on the Mount introduces a series of essential discourses recorded in Matthew. This sermon is a masterful exposition of the law and a potent assault on Pharisaic legalism, closing with a call to authentic faith and salvation (7:13-29).

Christ expounded the whole meaning of the law, showing that its demands were humanly impossible (5:48). This is the proper use of the law concerning salvation.

It closes off every possible avenue of human merit and leaves sinners dependent on nothing but divine grace for salvation (Rom. 3:19-20; Gal. 3:23-24).

Christ plumbed the depth of the law, showing that its actual demands went far beyond the surface meaning of the words (5:28, 39,

44) and set a standard higher than the most diligent students of the law had previously realized (5:20).

Matthew 5:1-2 "And seeing the multitudes, he went up into a mountain: and when he was set, his disciples came unto him:" "And he opened his mouth, and taught them, saying,"

"He was set": This was the normal posture for rabbis while teaching sitting.

Let me set the scene for you before we begin. This mountain, spoken of here, was probably a high area next to the Sea of Galilee. By land, it would, presumably, be between Tiberias and Capernaum.

A multitude thronged Jesus. Many followed Him because of the miracles. He did not exclude these people from the teaching. He just drew aside to an area where the disciples could sit closer for His education (whether twelve or more, we do not know; it was probably many more).

The multitude could listen and glean from His words if they were to the point where they could understand this profound teaching. In most instances, these people were familiar with the law.

The statement *"when he was set"* means that He sat down amid them to teach. They were eager to hear His teachings. It was more teaching than preaching. The statement

"He opened his mouth" means that this was not for casual conversation but rather deliberate teaching on Jesus' part.

The location is now called the Mount of Beatitudes. A church has been erected to mark the place believed to be where this message came from.

The Sermon on the Mount is the most excellent teaching of all time. If we could truly understand in depth what Jesus is saying, we would be able to discern the entire Bible from this.

Let's remember that all the Scriptures in this lesson, beginning with (Matthew 5:3), are printed in red in the Bible. They are the spoken Word of Jesus Christ Himself.

Matthew 5:3: "Blessed are the poor in spirit: for theirs is the kingdom of heaven."

"Blessed" means "happy, fortunate, blissful," and it speaks of more than a surface emotion. Jesus was describing the divinely bestowed well-being that belongs only to the faithful. It is a basic description of the believers' inner condition because of the work of God.

The Beatitudes prove that the way to heavenly blessedness is antithetical to the worldly path typically followed in pursuit of happiness. The Beatitudes give Jesus a description of the character of true faith.

These Beatitudes, like Psalm 1, do not show a man how to be saved but rather describe the characteristics of one who has been saved. The *"poor in spirit"* are the opposite of the proud or haughty in spirit. The opposite of self-sufficiency speaks of the profound humility of recognizing one's utter spiritual bankruptcy apart from God.

It describes those acutely:

conscious of their lostness,

 hopelessness apart from divine grace.

The grace of God has humbled them, and they have acknowledged their sin and, therefore, their dependence upon God to save them.

They will inherit the *"kingdom of heaven."* The Kingdom of Heaven is a general designation of the dwelling place of the saved.

First, let us look at the *BE Attitude.* What would we be? Jesus is saying in this very first verse of the Sermon on the Mount, can't you understand that you are not self-sufficient?

Your spirit is unlearned and dependent on the Spirit of God. You are poor in spirit compared to the wealth of God's Spirit. Depend on God, and not on self.

It directly opposed the Jewish leaders, who thought they knew everything because they had the law. The one thing we want to receive in this is that our wealth of spiritual knowledge depends on our faith in God's Spirit.

"Theirs is the kingdom of heaven": Notice that the truth of salvation by grace is presupposed in this opening verse of the Sermon on the Mount. Jesus taught that the kingdom is a gracious gift to those who sense their poverty of spirit.

Matthew 5:4 "Blessed are they that mourn: for they shall be comforted."

It speaks of mourning over sin, the godly sorrow that produces repentance, leading to salvation without regret (2 Cor. 7:10). The *"comfort"* is the comfort of forgiveness and salvation.

Those *that "mourn … shall be comforted."* The depth of the promise of these statements is almost inexhaustible. Those who mourn for sin shall be comforted in confession.

The compassion of God shall settle those who mourn for the human anguish of the lost.

There are two ways to look at this statement. In the physical, we mourn for our dead, and indeed, we will be comforted on that great day when we meet Jesus and our loved ones in the sky. Humanity's mourning can be turned into joy.

There is another way to look at this, as well. When we think of our sins, we are grieved and mourn. Our comfort comes in knowing we are forgiven.

We mourn for those out of fellowship with God. Whether relatives or friends have not made peace with God. Our prayers for them do not go unnoticed. Even in this life, our comfort will come as they come into the Church of Jesus Christ. No one likes the idea of mourning, but when it brings us to salvation, how glorious it is!

Matthew 5:5 Blessed are the meek: for they shall inherit the earth."

"The meek … shall inherit the earth" refers to those who have been humbled before God and will not only inherit the blessedness of heaven but will ultimately share in the kingdom of God on earth.

Here, in the opening statements of the Sermon on the Mount, is the balance between the physical and spiritual promise of the kingdom. The kingdom of which Jesus preached is both "in you" and is yet "to come."

The word *"meek"* has been misunderstood by so many. It means humble or mild-mannered. It is the opposite of being out of control. It is not weakness, but supreme self-control empowered by the Spirit (Gal. 5:23).

It is an attitude of the soul toward God and man, being willing to be instructed by God and ready to receive chastisement when necessary.

It has nothing to do with going around with your head hanging down or even allowing people to push you around. It is a humble heart, quick to understand, forgive, and obey God. We see here a blessing connected with it.

"Inherit the earth": Christians will reign with Jesus as his subordinates here on the earth during the 1,000-year reign of Christ, and we indeed shall inherit the earth. It is just another attribute of the Christian's humble heart.

Matthew 5:6: "Blessed are they which do hunger and thirst after righteousness: for they shall be filled."

These future possessors of the earth are its presently installed rightful heirs, and even now, they *"hunger and thirst after righteousness."* This is the opposite of the self-righteousness of the Pharisees.

It speaks of those who seek God's righteousness rather than attempting to establish their righteousness (Rom 10:3; Phil. 3:9).

What they seek will fill them, i.e., satisfy their hunger and thirst for a right relationship with God. They experience a deep desire for personal righteousness, proof of their spiritual rebirth.

Those who are poor and empty in their spiritual poverty recognize the depth of their need, hunger, and thirst for what only God can give them. *"They shall be filled"* (Greek *chorizo*) refers to complete satisfaction. The psalmist proclaimed: "*He satisfied the longing soul and filled the hungry soul with goodness" (Psalm 107:9).*

This verse needs very little explanation. Those trying to be in the right standing with God (righteousness) spend much time studying God's Word. The more we seek and consume the Word, the more we are complete. The only way we can be blessed is to know that these blessings are available and how to act upon them. God's Word reveals the blessings.

Matthew 5:7: "Blessed are the merciful: for they shall obtain mercy."

Those who are "*merciful … shall obtain mercy*" have reference to those who have been born again by the mercy of God. Because divine love is stretched out to them, they have the work of the Holy Spirit in them, producing an understanding that defies explanation by unregenerate men.

Jesus Himself became the ultimate example when He cried from the cross, "*Father, forgive them; for they know not what they do" (Luke 23:34).*

We reap what we sow. *The Lord tells us that He will forgive our trespasses, as we forgive those who trespass against us (Mark 11:25-26).*

My cry is not for a just God but a merciful one. Our just reward is death, but through the mercy of God, we are saved by His grace.

Matthew 5:8: "Blessed are the pure in heart: for they shall see God."

"See God": Not only with the feeling of faith but in the glory of heaven (Heb. 12:14; Rev. 22:3-4).

I am so happy that this Scripture does not say pure in deeds. The Lord will judge our hearts on judgment day. I have said so many times that if we are genuinely saved, we no longer have the desire in our hearts to sin. Old things and desires have passed; behold, all things become new.

It is our heart that has been made new. The Bible says for the mouth to speak out of the abundance of the heart. There is a spiritual seeing of God for the present when our hearts are pure, and there will be a physical seeing of God when we join Him in heaven.

Those who are not pure in heart will spend an eternity in hell and will not be with God as the Christians will be.

Matthew 5:9: "Blessed are the peacemakers: for they shall be called the children of God."

The following description deals with *the "peacemakers."* They are at peace with God and desire to live in harmony with all men (Rom. 5:1).

Their peace with Christ enables them to be ambassadors of God's message to a troubled world. Hence, they shall be called "the children of God."

Throughout the Beatitudes, Jesus underscores that only those who have the qualities of a changed life, herein described, are citizens of His kingdom.

Jesus is the King of Peace. The only true peace comes from Him. There will never be peace on the earth until the King of Peace comes and brings His peace to the planet.

If we are His children, we pattern our lives by His; we also bring peace around us as He has given us His peace within. Indeed, we are His children (followers) in His peace.

Matthew 5:10: "Blessed are they which are persecuted for righteousness' sake: for theirs is the kingdom of heaven."

As Jesus develops His message, He teaches that such a life causes His people to be in direct contrast to the world in which they live.

Therefore, He reminds us, *"Blessed are they which are persecuted for righteousness" sake."* The plural use of *"ye"* (in verse 11) shows that He foresaw this persecution as touching all His followers.

2 Timothy 3:12, "Yea, and all that will live godly in Christ Jesus shall suffer persecution."

To be persecuted for something we have done wrong is one thing, but to be persecuted because we are, to the best of our ability, serving God is something else.

Paul said to count it all joy when we are persecuted for Jesus. The disciples and Paul thought it a great honor to be persecuted for preaching about Jesus.

Most ministers today are not under persecution. Many are preaching what their congregation wants to hear. They are careful not to stir up the regular members by preaching against adultery, homosexuality, stealing, lying, coveting, and all the other sins of our day.

If you start preaching hard against pornography, rock music, drugs, alcohol, X-rated and PG-rated television and movies, and a total lapse of fellowship with God, you will see persecution.

People do not want to be preached about their sins. It is okay to preach about sins they are not committing. Just don't preach on "their" sins.

Many of the early Christians are martyred in the name of Jesus Christ. Are we that committed today and would proclaim Jesus even to the death?

With God's help, I will preach what I hear in my spirit for the church. We must repent and renew our lives with the Lord Jesus Christ. Heaven is our home. We are just here temporarily.

The Scripture says when we see significant troubles coming upon the earth to look up and rejoice (Luke 21:28), "And when these things begin to come to pass, then look up, and lift your heads; for your redemption draws near.

Matthew 5:11-12 "Blessed are ye, when men shall revile you, and persecute you, and shall say all manner of evil against you falsely, for my sake."

"*Rejoice* and be exceeding glad: for great is your reward in heaven: for so persecuted they the prophets which were before you." Rejoice" is the command that grows out of the believer's blessedness.

The phrases "Rejoices" and "be exceeding glad" mean even more, exult! "Great is your reward in heaven" focuses attention on the eternal destiny of all things.

If God is as correct as He claims, if the Bible is true, if heaven is to be gained, then no temporary earthly trouble or persecution can dispossess the child of God of joy in the prospect of the eternal glory that lies ahead.

They persecuted Jesus because He didn't fit into their pattern. They will persecute the followers of Jesus for the same reason. If you are not under persecution, you better take your spiritual pulse; something is probably wrong.

There is a great shaking in the true church today; only those who are indeed sold out to Jesus will stand.

Matthew 5:13: "Ye are the salt of the earth: but if the salt has lost his savor, wherewith shall it be salted? It is thenceforth good for nothing but to be cast out and trodden under the foot of men."

The Beatitudes are followed by a summary statement of the essential character of the Christian's life as salt and light. "Ye are the salt of the earth:" Again, the phrase "ye are" indicates that only the genuinely born-again person is salt and can help meet the world's needs.

Salt adds flavoring, is a preservative, melts coldness, and heals wounds. Thus, it is a very appropriate description of the believer in his relationship to the world in which he lives.

Salt is a preservative. Christians are a preservative. This earth would already have been destroyed if it were not for the few Christians here. If the Christians fall away, what will happen to the planet?

That is just precisely what is happening today. Watered-down Christianity is taking over. If the Christians do not raise a standard, then all is lost.

Lukewarm Christians will not make the final cut. God will spew lukewarm Christians out like lukewarm water. We need to live by the standards raised in the Bible. Sold out to God, Christians are the salt of the earth. We must preserve the Bible and its ideals until Jesus returns. We must not compromise with the world.

Chapter 4

The Ten Commandments

Deuteronomy 5:1 – 11:32: As Moses began his second address to the people of Israel, he reminded them of the events and the basic commands from God that were foundational to the Sinaitic Covenant (5:1-33; Exodus 19:1 – 20:21).

Then (6:1 – 11:32), Moses expounded and applied the first three of the Ten the Ten Commandments to the present experience of the people.

Verses 1-5: The summons to obey the law begins the "the Ten Commandments to the present experience of the people.

<u>*Verses 1-5:*</u> The summons to obey the law begins the "covenant stipulations" section in an ancient Near Eastern suzerainty overlordship treaty.

<u>*"Hear, O Israel"*</u> is repeated (in 4:1; 6:3-4; 9:1; 20:3; 27:9) to mark the beginning of a new appeal for obedience on the part of Israel. The verb carries the sense of "obey.

" A proper hearing implies that <u>*ye may learn them, keep, and do them."*</u> Knowledge is a prerequisite to performance.

Moses demands attention. When we hear the word of God, we must learn it, and what we have learned we must put into practice, for that is the end of hearing and learning.

Not to fill our heads with notions or our mouths with talk but to direct our affections and conduct.

Deuteronomy 5:1: "And Moses called all Israel, and said unto them, Hear, O Israel, the statutes and judgments which I speak in your ears this day, that ye may learn them, and keep, and do them."

"Hear, O Israel": The verb "hears" carried the sense "obey." All the people demanded a hearing that leads to obedience (6:4; 9:1; 20:3; 27:9).

Moses has called all the people together for a re-stating of the law. The law was first given at Horeb, where the voice of God came from the fire. Moses knows that many of those who were present that day are dead.

The forty years in the wilderness have caused many older people to die. Moses will repeat the law and judgments to them again so they will be without excuse.

Deuteronomy 5:2: "The Lord our God made a covenant with us in Horeb."

"A covenant with us in Horeb": The second generation of Israel, while children, received the covenant God made with Israel at Sinai.

Moses at once explains who God is. He is every individual's personal Lord and God.

The covenant Jesus made with the people was conditional. If they keep His commandments, He will bless them. If they do not mark them, He will curse them.

Deuteronomy 5:3: "The Lord made not this covenant with our fathers, but with us, even us, who are all of us here alive this day."

"Made not this covenant with our fathers": The "fathers" were not the people's immediate fathers, who had died in the wilderness, but their more distant ancestors, the patriarchs (4:31, 37; 7:8, 12; 8:18).

The Sinaitic or Mosaic Covenant was in addition to and distinct from the Abrahamic Covenant made with the patriarchs.

The covenant is for the living, not for the dead. It is the covenant God made with them as a people at Mount Sinai. The nation of Israel had gone into agreement with God. The older people who were involved in that agreement are dead.

Moses, Caleb, and Joshua remain the leaders who met with the Lord at Sinai. The covenant was not made with individuals but with the nation. This new generation is now Israel. The covenant, then, is with them.

Deuteronomy 5:4 "The Lord talked with you face to face in the mount out of the midst of the fire,"

Meaning, not in that accessible, friendly, and familiar manner, he sometimes talked with Moses, of whom this phrase is used (Exodus 33:11). But publicly, audibly, clearly, and distinctly, or without the interposition of another.

He did not speak to them by Moses but to them themselves. He talked to them without a middle person between them, as Aben Ezra expresses it. Without using one to relate to them what he said, he spoke to them directly, personally.

"Out of the midst of the fire": In which he descended, and with which the mountain was burning all the time he spoke. Which made it awful and pointed at the terrors of the legal dispensation.

Moses had gathered the people to the side of the mountain, and God had spoken to them from the fire on the hill.

Deuteronomy 5:5: "I stood between the Lord and you at that time, to shew you the word of the Lord: for ye were afraid because of the fire, and went not up into the mount;) saying,"

Between the Word of the Lord and you, as the Targums of Onkelos and Jonathan.

That is, about that time, not at the exact precise time the Ten Commandments were delivered, for these were spoken at once to the people.

But when the ceremonial law was given, which was ordained by angels, in the hand of a mediator (Gal. 3:19). And which was at the request of the people as follows, terrified by the appearance of the fire out of which the moral law was delivered.

"To show you the word of the Lord": Not the Decalogue, that they heard with their ears, but the other laws which were of the ceremonial and judicial kind.

"For ye were afraid because of the fire and went not up into the mount": Lest they should be consumed by it. And indeed, bounds were set about the mount, and they were charged not to break through.

"Saying": This word is in connection with the preceding verse, the Lord's talking out of the midst of the fire when he said what follows.

The following verses show the people's fear of the Lord and that Moses spoke to God for them.

Exodus 20:18-19 "And all the people saw the thundering, and the flashes of lightning, and the noise of the trumpet, and the mountain smoking: and when the people saw it, they removed, and stood afar off." "And they said unto Moses, Speak thou with us, and we will hear but let not God speak with us, lest we die."

Verses 6-22: There is some variation from (Exodus 20), as between the Lord's prayer in (Matt. 6 and Luke 11). We need to tie ourselves to the things more than the words unalterably. The original reason for hallowing the Sabbath, taken from God's resting from the work of creation on the seventh day, is not here mentioned. Though this stays in force, it is not the only reason.

Here, it is taken from Israel's deliverance out of Egypt, for that was typical of our redemption by Jesus Christ, in remembrance of which the Christian Sabbath was to be seen and in the resurrection of Christ, brought into the glorious liberty of the children of God with a mighty hand and an outstretched arm.

How sweet is it to a soul truly distressed under the terrors of a broken law to hear the mild and soul-reviving language of the gospel!

Verses 6-21: The first four commandments involve a relationship with God, and the last six deal with human relationships; together, they were the foundation of Israel's life before God.

Moses here reiterated them as given originally at Sinai—Moses' explanatory purpose in Deuteronomy accounts for slight variations in the Exodus text. Exodus 20:1-17 for an added explanation of these commands. The commands to love God and others summarize the Ten Commandments and reflect His holy character (Matt. 22:37-40).

Verses 6-10: This section has the first and second commandments and relates to the worship of God.

"I am the Lord thy God, which brought thee out of the land of Egypt, from the house of bondage" is a phrase that appears over one hundred- twenty-five times in the Old Testament.

Usually, this reminder went along with a command or ethical demand. The context or environment of law and obligation in the Old Testament period was the redemption of Israel from Egypt.

The Lawgiver and His gracious act of redemption provide the context against which the commandments are given. *"Before me":*

The highest duty of man is shown in the first commandment. *"Image":* There are fourteen Hebrew words for idols or images; this probably refers to "gods of silver or gods of gold" (Exodus 20:23), as well as those carved from stone, wood, and those later made from metal.

"Likeness": Resemblance" or *"form"* applies to any real or imagined pictorial representation of deities. It's not intended to stifle artistic talent, for the command references religious worship.

God commanded Moses to make many artistic representations on the curtains in the Tabernacle.

"Jealous": This must not be construed to mean that God is naturally suspicious, wrongfully envious of the success of others, or distrustful.

When used of God, it refers to:

- The quality in His character that demands exclusive devotion.

- The attribute of anger that He directs against all who oppose Him; and

- He spends the energy on the justification of His people.

"Mercy" (chesed) implies an unfailing love that is grounded in the covenant and is used both for God's attitude toward His people and for the response He wants from them (1 John 4:11, 19), the latter occurring mainly in Hosea.

It is always closely connected with the two concepts of covenant and faithfulness.

Deuteronomy 5:6: "I am the LORD thy God, which brought thee out of the land of Egypt, from the house of bondage."

The Ten Commandments are the same as those in Exodus 20:2.

Those commands are here delivered in the same order and near in the exact words, with a bit of variation and a few additions.

Which I shall only see and refer to (Exodus 20:1) for the sense of the various laws.

He is the great I AM: He is the One who eternally exists. It was God that brought them out of Egypt. Moses led them under the direction of the LORD. The rules for all men to live by must come from God. Man's law is not unfailing.

Deuteronomy 5:7: "Thou shalt have none other gods before me."

"No other gods": Exodus 20:3. "Other gods" were non-existent pagan gods, made in the form of idols and shaped by the minds of their worshipers. The Israelite was to be faithful to the God to whom he was bound by covenant (Matt. 16:24-27; Mark 8:34-38; Luke 9:23-26; 14:26-33).

It is the first of the *Ten Commandments*. We see in this very first commandment that there is One God. The worship of false gods would break the first commandment of God.

Deuteronomy 5:8 "Thou shalt not make thee any graven image, or any likeness of anything that is in heaven above, or that is in the earth beneath, or that is in the waters beneath the earth:"

"Any graven image … any likeness" (Exodus 20:4-5). Reducing the infinite God to any physical likeness was intolerable, as the people found out in their attempt to cast God as a golden calf (Exodus chapter 32).

Any image would not be God. God is Spirit.

John 4:24: "God is a Spirit: and they that worship him must worship him in spirit and truth."

Graven images are idol worship.

Verses 9-10: "The third and fourth generations … thousands" (Exodus 20:5-6, for an explanation of this often-misunderstood text).

"Them that hate me … Them that love me": Disobedience is equal to hatred of God, as love is equal to obedience (Matt. 22:34-40; Rom. 13:8-10).

Deuteronomy 5:9 "Thou shalt not bow down thyself unto them, nor serve them: for I the LORD thy God am a jealous God, visiting the iniquity of the fathers upon the children unto the third and fourth generation of them that hate me,"

It is the preface to the Ten Commandments and is the same as that in (Exodus 20:2; Exodus 20:2). And those commands are here delivered in the same order, and near in the exact words, with a bit of variation, and a few additions. Which I shall only see and refer to (Exodus 20:1) for the sense of the various laws.

"Visiting the iniquity of the fathers upon the children": No sins entail penal consequences upon succeeding generations as the abominations of idolatry. *All idolatry means the degradation of the Divine image in man.* But it is not represented here that the son's soul shall die for the father. The penalty extends only *"to them that hate me."*

We know the heathen women had easily influenced the Jews to bow down to their false gods. It is the one sin that God will not overlook.

It is spiritual adultery when they are unfaithful to God, strictly forbidden.

Deuteronomy 5:10: "And showing mercy unto thousands of them that love me and keep my commandments."

"Them that love me":

We have an echo of this commandment in the words of our Savior: *"If ye love me, keep my commandments"* (John 14:15).

The promise of His presence with us through the "other Comforter" compensates for the absence of any visible image. As love in this verse is practical, so is hatred in the earlier verse.

To hate God is to disobey His commandments.

The mercy of God is forever.

Deuteronomy 7:9: "Know therefore that the Lord thy God, he is God, the faithful God, which keep covenant and mercy with them that love him and keep his commandments to a thousand generations;"

James 5:11: "Behold, we count them happy which endure. Ye have heard of the patience of Job and have seen the end of the Lord; that the Lord is very pitiful and of tender mercy."

Deuteronomy 5:11: "Thou shalt not take the name of the Lord thy God in vain: for the Lord will not hold him guiltless that taketh his name in vain."

"Take the name … in vain" (Exodus 20:7). Attach God's name to emptiness (Psalm 111:9; Matt. 6:9; Luke 1:49; John 17:6, 26).

This verse relates to the third commandment. The meaning is to "misuse" God's name or use it for no real purpose. Examples may be:

- To affirm something false and untrue.

- To express mild surprise; and

- ☒To use His name when there is no clear goal, purpose, or reason for its use in the context, such as in a prayer of another religious context.

It is speaking of all profanity that uses the name of the Lord. It is strictly forbidden to misuse the name of the Lord.

James 5:12: "But above all things, my brethren, swear not, neither by heaven, neither by the earth, neither by any other oath: but let your yea be yea; and your nay, nay; lest ye fall into condemnation."

What comes out of the mouth begins in the heart.

Those who profane the name of the LORD have profanity in their hearts.

Verses 12-15: These verses relate to the fourth commandment. It was given for the individual's liberation, not the bondage.

It was for *"rest"*. Another reason is shown here, relating to the nation's creation when they were redeemed from Egypt. Because of this new work of redemption, they are to rest.

Deuteronomy 5:12: "Keep the sabbath day to sanctify it, as the Lord thy God hath commanded thee."

"As the Lord thy God hath commanded thee" (exodus 20:8-10). These words are missing from Exodus 20:8 but refer to this commandment given to Israel at Sinai forty years earlier.

Or see it by setting it apart as a time of natural rest and for the performance of holy and religious exercises, where the phrase is a little varied, *"remember the Sabbath day to keep it holy"*; it has been instituted before.

"As the Lord thy God hath commanded thee": Not at Sinai only, for the same might then have been seen of all the rest of the commands, but before the giving of the law, at the first of the manna (see Exodus 16:23).

The Sabbath is the seventh day of the week or Saturday. Those under the law must practice Sabbath or Saturday.

Deuteronomy 5:13 "Six days thou shalt labor, and do all thy work:"

The appeal to see the Sabbath and allow time of rest to servants (Exodus 23:12) Is pointed to by reminding the people that they were formerly servants.

The bondage in Egypt and the deliverance from it are not assigned as grounds for the institution of the Sabbath, which is of far older date (Genesis 2:3).

But rather as suggesting motives for the religious observance of that institution.

The Exodus was an entrance into rest from the toils of the house of bondage and is thought to have occurred on the Sabbath day or *"rest"* day.

The Sabbath is a time for rest. Jesus said it best in the following Scripture.

Mark 2:27 "And he said unto them, the Sabbath was made for man, and not man for the sabbath:"

Man is to work six days and rest one day.

Deuteronomy 5:14 "But the seventh day is the sabbath of the Lord thy God: in it thou shalt not do any work, thou, nor thy son, nor thy daughter, nor thy manservant, nor thy maidservant, nor thine ox, nor thine ass, nor any of thy cattle, nor thy stranger that is within thy gates; that thy manservant and thy maidservant may rest as well as thou."

In (Exodus 20:10), it is only in general said.

"Nor thy cattle": Here, by illustration and explanation, the ox and the ass are particularly mentioned. One is used in plowing ground, treading out the corn, and the other in carrying burdens, and it is added.

"Nor any of thy cattle": As their camels, or whatever else they were accustomed to use in any service. There were none of them to do any work on the Sabbath day. The following clause has not been used before, expressing this institution's end.

"That thy manservant and maidservant may have rest as well. If the cattle had not rested, they could not have, being obliged to attend them at the plow or elsewhere. And this respects not only hired but bondservants and maidens.

The Sabbath is a time set aside from all physical labor. It is a time of refreshing in the Lord. Every man and animal needs time to rest their body and their mind. This time was set aside for man by the Lord to give him a refreshing time. Even though this day is set aside for worship, it is for the benefit of man.

Deuteronomy 5:15: "And remember that thou were a servant in the land of Egypt and that the Lord thy God brought thee out thence through a mighty hand and by a stretched-out arm: therefore, the Lord thy God commanded thee to keep the sabbath day."

"Brought thee out forward": Here, an added reason is given for God's rest after creation *for the observance of the Sabbath* (Exodus 20:11), God's deliverance of the people from Egypt.

While the Israelites had been enslaved people in Egypt, they were not allowed rest from their continual labor, so the Sabbath was also to function as a day of rest in which their deliverance from bondage would be remembered with thanksgiving as the sign of their redemption and continual sanctification (Exodus 31:13-17; Ezek. 20:12).

"Remember that thou were a bondman": Similar words are used in Deuteronomy to encourage the people to the proper behavior expected of them (5:15; 10:19; 16:12; and 24:18, 22). As "Children of the Lord" (14:1), they should bear His character.

This day of rest (Sabbath) is not an option but a commandment of the Lord. God rested from His labors, and man is to rest one day in seven from his works.

Verses 16-20:(Matt. 19:18:19; Mark 10:19; Luke 18:20).

Deuteronomy 5:16: "Honor thy father and thy mother, as the Lord thy God hath commanded thee; that thy days may be prolonged, and that it may go well with thee, in the land which the Lord thy God giveth thee."

This verse relates to authority, with the sanctity of the family in mind. Honor involves:

- Prizing them highly (Prov. 4:8).

- Caring and showing affection to them (Psalm 91:15).

- Showing them respect, reverence, and deference (Lev. 19:3).

"That thy days may be prolonged" (Exodus 20:12; Matt. 15:4; Mark 7:10; Eph. 6:2-3).

Paul showed that this was the first commandment with a promise attached (Eph. 6:2).

Jesus also had much to say about honoring parents (Matt. 10:37; 19:29; Luke 2:49-51; John 19:26-27).

Ephesians 6:1 says that "obedience" is to be "in the Lord".

Parents are to be honored, but never should their wishes or words become a rival or substitute for the Will or Word of God.

Families who heed this command honor the Lord and strengthen society, producing good citizens and leaders.

A reward for children is also offered: *"honor" your parents,* and God will honor you with a longer life (Eph. 6:2-3). *The practice of honor is respect.*

Matthew 15:4: "For God commanded, saying, honor thy father and mother: and He that cursed father or mother, let him die the death."

Our father and mother are responsible for our birth. God gives us life. He uses our fathers and mothers to bring us to life.

We should greatly respect the parents who brought us into the world. God should be first in our lives, but we should have regard for our parents.

Deuteronomy 5:17 "Thou shalt not kill."

This verse relates to the sanctity of life. The Hebrew language has seven words related to "kill." This word is almost always used for killing a personal enemy (ratsah) but is not confined to intentional and premeditated murder.

The prohibition applies to:

- Suicide:

- To all accessories to the murder (2 Sam. 12:9); and

- To all those who have the authority of a magistrate or governor but do not use it to punish known and convicted murderers (1 Kings 21:19).

At least nineteen crimes were calling for the death penalty in the Old Testament:

- Premediated murder

- kidnapping,

- adultery,

- homosexuality,

- incest,

- bestiality,

- incorrigible delinquency,

- persistent disobedience to parents and authorities,

- striking or cursing parents,

- offering human sacrifice,

- false prophecy,

- blasphemy,

- profaning the Sabbath,

- sacrificing to false gods,

- magic,

- divination,

- unchastity,

- rape of a betrothed virgin.

- Only for the first crime, premeditated murder, was no ransom or substituted acceptable (Num. 35:31).

I am speaking of premeditated murder.

Deuteronomy 5:18: "Neither shalt thou commit adultery."

This verse relates to adultery and the sanctity of marriage. It was punishable by death and was distinguished from fornication (Exodus 22:16; Deut. 22:28-29).

Exodus 20:14; Matt. 5:27.

Adultery, in the physical sense, is taking part in sex with someone you are not married to. In the spiritual sense, adultery is speaking of the worship of false gods.

Cheating of all kinds is strictly forbidden.

Deuteronomy 5:19: "Neither shalt thou steal."

This verse relates to theft and the sanctity of property.

The Old Testament taught that God owned everything in heaven and on earth (Psalm 24:1; 115:16) and that He has only entrusted it to others. Thus, theft was stealing from God as well as from man.

(Exodus 20:15; Eph. 4:28).

To take anything that does not belong to you is stealing. Employees even steal from their employers when they do not give them a full day's work for a full day's pay.

Deuteronomy 5:20: "Neither shalt thou bear false witness against thy neighbor."

This *ninth commandment* is related to false charges and the sanctity of truth. It applied to all areas of life, even though the terminology reflects the legal process in Israel, *"false witness."*

To despise the fact was to hate God, whose very being was the truth. *"Lying"* (Hosea 4:2) shows the commandment had a broad application.

Exodus 20:16; Col. 3:9.

It is a ruthless thing to do. It does not build your position up to tear someone else down. We must always speak the truth if we are believers in the Lord. We should build our neighbors up and not tear them down.

Deuteronomy 5:21 "Neither shalt thou desire thy neighbor's wife, neither shalt thou covet thy neighbor's house, his field, his manservant, or his maidservant, his ox, or his ass, or anything that is thy neighbor's."

The sanctity of motives is presented in the final commandment.

It relates to an inner quality of contentment. *"Desire"* (chamad), "to desire earnestly," *"to long after,"* and "to covet" are used in (Genesis 3:6), as they relate to the tree and its ability to make one wise.

The word *"covet"* (awah) also means to *set one's desire for something, such as food.*

Relates *to the inner instinct that lies behind all acts, thoughts, and words* (Matt. 15:19; Mark 7:21; Luke 12:15; Rom. 1:24; 2 Cor. 9:5; Eph. 5:3; and 1 Tim. 6:6):

"Godliness with contentment is great gain."

The tenth commandment prohibited lusting after a neighbor's wife and a strong desire for a neighbor's property (Rom. 7:7).

We should rejoice in the fact that our neighbor has these things. It is coveting to want anything that belongs to someone else.

Luke 12:15: "And he said unto them, take heed, and beware of covetousness: for a man's life consistent not in the abundance of the things which he possessed."

All the Ten Commandments are covered in the following two that Jesus gave.

Matthew 22:37-39 "Jesus said unto him, thou shalt love the Lord thy God with all thy heart, and with all thy soul, and with all thy mind." "This is the first and great commandment." "And the second is like unto it, thou shalt love thy neighbor as thyself."

God first, spouse, children, parents, neighbor second, and yourself third covers all the Ten Commandments.

Verses 22-27: The frightening circumstances of God's presence at Sinai caused the people to have enough fear to ask Moses to receive the words from God and communicate those words to them, after which they promised to obey all that God said (verse 27).

Deuteronomy 5:22: "These words the Lord spoke unto all your assembly in the mount out of the midst of the fire, of the cloud, and of the thick darkness, with a great voice: and he added no more. And he wrote them in two tables of stone and delivered them unto me."

"And he added no more": These Ten Commandments alone were identified as direct quotations by God.

The rest of the covenant stipulations were given to Moses, who, in turn, gave them to the Israelites.

These basic rules, which reflect God's character, continue to be a means by which God reveals the sinful deeds of the flesh (Rom. 7:7-14; Gal. 3:19-24; 5:13-26).

They are also a holy standard from conduct that the saved live by through the Spirit's power, apart from keeping the Sabbath (Col. 2:16-17).

"*Two tables of stone*": The tables were written on both sides (Exodus 32:15).

The same message was spoken to the people that the message the fiery finger of God wrote on the tablets.

They are the Decalogue or the Ten Commandments.

"Decalogue" means ten words.

Verses 23-33: Moses refers to the consternation caused by the terror with which the law was given. God's appearances have been terrible to man ever since the fall, but Christ, having taken away sin, invites us to come boldly to the throne of grace.

They were in a sound mind, under the strong convictions of the words they heard. Many have their consciences startled by the law who have them not purified.

Fair promises are extorted from them, but no sound principles are fixed and rooted in them. God commended what they said. He wants the welfare and salvation of poor sinners.

He has given abundant proof that he does so; he gives us time and space to repent. He has sent his Son to redeem us, promised his Spirit to those who pray for him, and declared that he has no pleasure in the ruin of sinners.

It would be well with many if there were always such a heart in them as there seems to be sometimes. When they are under conviction of sin or the rebukes of providence, or when they come to look death in the face.

The only way to be happy is to be holy. Say to the righteous, it shall be well with them. Let believers make it more and more their study and delight more to do as the Lord God has commanded.

Verses 23-27: God is so holy that the Israelites thought that even hearing His "voice" could mean their death (Exodus 20:18-19).

Deuteronomy 5:23: "And it came to pass, when ye heard the voice out of the midst of the darkness, for the mountain did burn with fire, that ye came near unto me, even all the heads of your tribes, and your elders;"

The thick darkness, where God was, and with which the mountain was covered (Exodus 20:21).

"For the mountain did burn with fire": This is why the Lord spoke out of the midst of the fire, the mountain he descended burning with it, and for his saying out of the midst of darkness.

Not only a thick cloud covered the mountain, but it was altogether on a smoke, which ascended as the smoke of a furnace (Exodus 19:16).

"That ye come near unto me, even all the heads of your tribes and your elders": Or wise men, as the Targum of Jonathan.

It appears that not only the ordinary people were frightened at what they heard and saw on Mount Sinai, but those of the first rank and eminence among them, who were the most famous for their authority and wisdom.

Moses had built a fence around the bottom of the mountain to keep them from touching the peak while the presence of God was on it.

If they had felt the mountain, they would have died. The fire, smoke, and the voice out of the fire were all they could stand. They ran back from the mountain when God began to speak in the fire.

Deuteronomy 5:24: "And ye said, Behold, the Lord our God hath showed us his glory and his greatness, and we have heard his voice out of the midst of the fire: we have seen this day that God doth talk with man, and he lived."

He descended on Mount Sinai as he did and gave the law from thence with such solemnity.

The apostle argues for the glory in its ministration (2 Cor. 3:7).

It delivered with so much majesty, and such a glorious apparatus attending it (see Deut. 33:2).

Aben Ezra interprets this as the appearance of fire in which the Lord was, "*and his greatness,*" of the thunders and flashes of lightning, and the voice of the trumpet.

"*And we have heard his voice out of the midst of the fire.*":

As the same interpreter rightly notes, the ten words were vocally and audibly expressed out of the fire.

"*We have seen this day that God does talk with man, and he lived.*":

They had proof of it in themselves; God had been talking with them out of the fire, yet it did not reach and consume them, but they were still alive.

God has revealed Himself to them, so they will realize these Ten Commandments are from Him, not Moses. They are amazed that any man can hear the voice of God and live.

Deuteronomy 5:25 "Now, therefore, why should we die? For this great fire will consume us: if we hear the voice of the Lord our God any more, then we shall die."

Since we are now alive and have so wonderfully escaped the danger, we were exposed to let us be careful that we are not liable to it again.

"*For this great fire will consume us*": If it continues, we are exposed to it. Perhaps some might remember the fire that burnt in the uttermost parts of the camp at Taberah.

And the destruction of Korah and the two hundred and fifty men with him by fire (Num. 11:1).

"If we hear the voice of the Lord our God any more, then we shall die," For it was such a voice of words they could not endure as to the matter of them.

And therefore, entreated, the term might not be spoken to them anymore: the killing letter and the ministration of condemnation and death.

And the way it was delivered was so terrible that they concluded they could not live but must die if they heard it again.

And imagined that if the fire continued, the flames of it would spread and reach them, and they would not be able to escape them.

God's presence is more than they can bear. Fear of death overwhelms them.

Deuteronomy 5:26: "For who is there of all flesh, that hath heard the voice of the living God speaking out of the midst of the fire, as we have, and lived?"

What man was there in any age that was ever heard of or can be named?

"That hath heard the voice of the living God": Who lives in and of himself and is the author and giver of life to all his creatures.

Whereby he is distinguished from and is opposed unto the lifeless deities of the Gentiles; and which makes him, and his voice heard the more awful and tremendous—and especially speaking out of the midst of the fire, which was the present case.

"As we have and lived?" Of this, there never was the like instance; for though some had seen God and lived, as Jacob did, and therefore called the name of the place where he saw him Penuel (Gen. 32:30).

And Moses had heard the voice of the angel of the Lord out of a bush, which seemed to be burning and was not consumed (Exodus 3:2).

Yet none ever heard the voice of the Lord out of the natural fire, and particularly expressing such words as he did, but the Israelites.

It does set them aside as extraordinary people. They are His chosen people.

It is not unnatural for men to fear the presence of God. Terror is a closer description than fear. They are amazed they are still alive.

Deuteronomy 5:27: "Go thou near and hear all that the Lord our God shall say: and speak thou unto us all that the Lord our God shall speak unto thee, and we will hear it and do it."

The mountain that God settled it.

And hear all that the Lord our God shall say": For they supposed, by the continuance of the Lord on the mount, and the fire burning on it, that he had more to say, which they were not averse to hear.

But wanted it might be not at once delivered to them, but by Moses—the sound of the words and the sight of the fire being so terrible to them.

"And speak thou unto us all that the Lord our God shall speak unto thee.":

They did not doubt, knowing the faithfulness of Moses, his declaring all unto them that the Lord should have told him.

And they were desirous that he should; they did not want anything withheld from them, only they could not bear to see and hear things at once from the Lord.

"And we will hear it and do it": Hearken to it, and receive it, as the word of God, not man. And yield ready and cheerful obedience, even to everything that should be needed. (Exodus 20:19).

They know now that Moses has a special relationship with the Lord. They ask Moses to communicate with God for them and then bring His message to them.

They promise to accept the message and do it.

Verses 28-29: God affirmed that the pledge to be obedient was the correct response (verse 28) and then expressed His loving passion for them to fulfill their promise so they and their children would prosper.

Verses 28–33: The people's response at this moment was so right before the Lord that Yahweh wistfully expressed sadness that they would not always respond in this manner (32:29).

Deuteronomy 5:28: "And the Lord heard the voice of your words when ye spoke unto me; and the Lord said unto me, I have heard the voice of the words of these people, which they have spoken unto thee: they have well said all that they have spoken."

Not only in general, but he also hears and knows all that men speak. For there is not a word on the tongue, formed upon and uttered by it, but what is altogether known to him.

But in a unique and particular manner, I saw, took notice of, approved, and was well pleased with what these people said.

"And the Lord said unto me, I have heard the voice of the words of this people which they have spoken unto thee":

Not only heard them but took notice of their sense and meaning and listened to them with pleasure and delight.

"They have well said all that they have spoken,"

Expressing such awe and reverence of the divine Majesty, wanting to have a mediator between God and them. And purposing and promising to listen to and obey whatsoever he should command by him.

The Lord heard them ask Moses to be their representative to Him. The Lord is pleased with that request. The Lord knows that speaking to them openly would cause problems for them.

Deuteronomy 5:29: "O that there was such a heart in them, that they would fear me, and keep all my commandments always, that it might be well with them, and with their children forever!"

It is spoken of God after the manner of men to show that such a heart is desirable to him and required by him.

Otherwise, it is inevitable that God can give such a heart and hath promised to provide it (Jer. 32:40; Ezek. 36:27). And if God will work, who can hinder him? (Job 11:10).

"That it might be well with them, and with their children forever":

For the fear of God, and the keeping of his commandments, issue in the good of men, in their interest, their inward peace, and spiritual welfare.

In the good of others, their neighbors, servants, and children, by example and instruction.

God knows their hearts and words were just promises they would not keep. As Moses goes up the mountain for forty days, they fall into great sin. The covenant depended upon them keeping God's commandments.

Verses 30-33: They asked to be assumed all God's Word (verse 27), so God dismissed the people and told Moses He would give the law to him to teach the people (verse 31).

At stake was life and prosperity in the Land of Promise.

Deuteronomy 5:30: "Go say to them, Get you into your tents again."

They had left, being brought by Moses, at the direction of God, to the foot of Mount Sinai to receive the law from his mouth.

They were well-ordered to return to their tents again, to their families, wives, and children.

They were to return to their tents while Moses communed with God for them. Moses would receive instructions from God for them and then deliver the message to the people.

Deuteronomy 5:31: "But as for thee, stand thou here by me, and I will speak unto thee all the commandments, and the statutes, and the judgments, which thou shalt teach them, that they may do them in the land which I give them to possess it."

On the mount by him whither he was called up. Moses was not allowed to go to his tent when the children of Israel were.

They lived to wait upon the Lord to receive his instructions, which he was to communicate to the people. Being a kind of a mediator between God and them, as they asked, and which had granted them.

"And I will speak unto thee all the commandments, statutes, and judgments."

All moral, ceremonial, and judicial laws belong to them as men, as in a church-state, and members of a body politic.

"Which thou shalt teach them, that they may do them":

All doctrine is to practice, without which all instructions and theoretical notions signify little. And these were more special to do, some of them peculiarly.

"In the land which I give them to possess it":

The land of Canaan laid on them no small obligation to do the commandments of God. Since of his free favor and goodwill, and as a pure gift of his, he had bestowed upon them a land flowing with milk and honey. Into which he was just now about to bring them.

Nothing can more strongly engage souls to cheerful obedience to the service of God, whether in private or in public, than the consideration of the great and good things which God of his rich grace bestows upon them.

He has promised to them, prepared for them, and will quickly put them into possession. And upon such an account, Moses presses the observance of the commands of God in the following verses.

God taught Moses His ways. He gave him the Ten Commandments and all the statutes and judgments for the people.

It was then Moses's commitment to introduce them to the people.

Exodus 24:3: "And Moses came and told the people all the words of the Lord, and all the judgments: and all the people answered with one voice, and said, All the words which the Lord had said will we do."

Deuteronomy 5:32: "Ye shall observe to do therefore as the Lord your God hath commanded you: ye shall not turn aside to the right hand or the left."

Observe every precept, as to matter and manner, which the Lord has commanded. And that under a sense of the outstanding obligations laid on them by him, in giving them freely so good a land to own.

"You shall not turn to the right hand or the left":

But walk in the way of the commandments of God, and not depart from them at all, but follow the Lord in his ways entirely.

The phrase is expressive of strict and close attention to the word of God without deviating from it.

Every sin, a transgression of some command of God or another, is a going out of the way that directs unto (Isaiah 30:21).

It is a warning from Moses:

That they must keep the commandments that God has sent them.

They must not wander out of the straight and narrow path He has set before them.

They are not to look to the world for answers. They must keep their eyes straight ahead on God.

Deuteronomy 5:33: "Ye shall walk in all the ways which the Lord your God hath commanded you, that ye may live, and that it may be well with you, and that ye may prolong your days in the land which ye shall possess."

None are to be avoided or left from on any consideration whatever (Psalm 119:6). An instance of this we have in Zacharias and Elizabeth (Luke 1:6).

That ye may live comfortably, in all the outward enjoyments of life needful for them, particularly in the possession of the land of Canaan and the benefits of it.

The promises of life upon obedience seem to reach no further unless as types and emblems of what is enjoyed through the observation and righteousness of Christ, as the following phrases show.

"And that it may be well with you, and that ye may prolong your days in the land ye shall possess."

The land of Canaan, though the Jewish writers carry it further, even to heaven and eternal happiness. And so may we in the sense before given.

God had promised to bless them on the earth in the land He had given them if they kept His commandments.

Ephesians 2:10: "For we are his workmanship, created in Christ Jesus unto good works, which God hath before ordained that we should walk in them."

Chapter 5

Salvation to the World

John 3:16: "For God so loved the world, that he gave his only begotten Son, that whosoever believeth in him should not perish, but have everlasting life."

Scripture in the entire Bible.

Acts 2:38 "Then Peter said unto them, Repent, and be baptized every one of you in the name of Jesus Christ for the remission of sins, and ye shall receive the gift of the Holy Ghost."

"Repent":

This refers to a change of mind and purpose that turns an individual from sin to God (1 Thess. 1:9). Such change involves more than fearing the consequences of God's judgment.

Genuine repentance knows that the evil of sin must be forsaken, and the person and work of Christ totally and singularly embraced.

Peter exhorted his hearers to repent, otherwise they would not experience true conversion (Matt. 3:2; Acts 3:19; 5:31; 8:22; 11:18; 17:30; 20:21; 26:20; Matt. 4:17).

"Be baptized":

This Greek word means *immersed" in water.* Peter was obeying Christ's command from (Matt. 28:19) and urging the people who repented and turned to the Lord Christ for salvation to show, through the waters of baptism, with His death, burial, and resurrection (Acts 19:5; Rom. 6:3-4; 1 Cor. 12:13; Gal. 3:27; see notes on Matt. 3:2).

It was the first time the apostles publicly joined the people to obey that ceremony.

Before this, many Jews had experienced the baptism of John the Baptist, (Matt. 3:1-3), and were also familiar with the baptism of Gentile converts to Judaism (proselytes).

"In the name of Jesus Christ":

For the new believer, it was a crucial but costly identification to accept.

"For the remission of sins":

This might better be translated as *"because of the forgiveness of sins".*

- Baptism does not produce forgiveness and cleansing from sin (1 Pet. 3:20-21).

- The reality of forgiveness precedes the rite of baptism (verse 41).

- Genuine repentance brings from God the forgiveness of sins (Eph. 1:7), and because of that the new believer was to be baptized.

Baptism,

However, was to be the ever-present act of obedience, so that it became identical to salvation.

Thus, to say one was baptized for forgiveness was the same as saying one was saved, *"one baptism"* in Eph. 4:5.

Every believer enjoys the complete forgiveness of sins (Matt. 26:28; Luke 24:47; Eph. 1:7; Col. 2:13; 1 John 2:12).

"The gift of the Holy Ghost" (1:5, 8).

Here, as throughout Scripture, one aspect of conversion is commonly used to be all aspects: believing and calling as well as repenting.

The grammatical name for allowing part of something to stand for the whole is called synecdoche.

- *Repentance: i*s something every person must do (17:30).

For several reasons *"be baptized"*, should not be joined with *"for the remission of sins"*, to teach baptismal renewal.

- First, the context of this passage proves that only repentance relates to the *removal of sin at salvation*: "*Whosoever shall call … shall be saved" (verse 21).* Peter's next recorded sermon states only *"Repent … that your sins may be blotted out" (3:19).*

- Second, throughout Acts men show their faith and salvation before baptism (10:43-47).

- Third, throughout the New Testament do include water baptism in the salvation experience (John 3:16; Acts 16:31; Romans 4:10; Eph. 2:1-10; 1 Pet. 1:18-19).

Thus, this verse more clearly reads, *"Repent for the remission of sins,* and you will receive the gift which is the Holy Spirit; and let each of you be baptized in the name of Christ."

Though water baptism does not save or wash away our sins, it is a command that needs to be obeyed speedily after conversion.

Jesus commanded it (Matt. 28:19-20), as does Peter here. This is the consistent pattern throughout Acts (16:31-34; 18:8).

These men Peter was speaking to here were the house of Israel. They had rejected Jesus as their Messiah.

They must repent of this rejection of Jesus as the substitute for their sin.

The one they had rejected is the very one they are to be baptized in the name of. These are all Jews here.

They must repent of rejecting Jesus. They had the law; the Gentiles did not have the law to go by.

The gift of the Holy Ghost would come after they had repented and been baptized. The part of those who want to be saved is to repent of their sin, and then believe in the name of Jesus.

Christ. Just as Abraham was justified just as if he had never sinned, by faith they will be justified by faith in Jesus Christ.

We read earlier how God will save all who call on His name.

You can easily see why because it is full of so much hope. We need to take a perfect look at it. "God so loved"; unconditional Love is a love so far above anything man knows that we do not understand.

The word love here is translated from Agape, which means to love much in a moral sense. This love goes way beyond the human ability to love. This type of love is not because but despite.

He loved us so much that while we were in sin, He sent His Son to die on the cross to save us, not because we deserved it, but because we didn't deserve it.

The Son's mission is bound up in the supreme love of God for the evil, sinful "world" of humanity that is in rebellion against Him.

The word *"so" emphasizes* the intensity or greatness of His love. The Father gave His unique and beloved Son to die for sinful men.

Jesus came to save the lost. It is so simple and yet so complex. Believeth here again continues to believe.

You see, salvation is a way of life. Every day, when we get up, we must remember all over again and think. It is not something we do casually. This belief means believing in God and loving Him more than anyone else.

Matthew 22:37: tells us what this love and belief is: "Jesus said unto him, thou shalt love the Lord thy God, with all thy heart, and with all thy soul, and with all thy mind."

If you believe, you will practice the verse above. God will be first in your life, or He will not be in your life at all. There is no way to perish if you are in this right standing with God. He has prepared us a place to spend eternity with Him.

John 3:17: "For God sent not his Son into the world to condemn the world; but that the world through him might be saved."

It "sent here" shows that Jesus is on a mission to accomplish His task forever. The name Jesus, as we have said before, means Redeemer or Jehovah Deliverer.

The Word took on the name of Jesus Christ for His work of salvation.

At the end of the age, there is a time when Jesus will be judged and determine each of our destinations, whether heaven or hell.

However, his mission to the earth was to save all humanity who would accept it. The name of Jesus is mighty.

The only way to get to heaven is through belief in Him. So, through Him, we receive eternal life.

John 3:18: "He that believeth on him is not condemned: but he that believeth not is condemned already, because he hath not believed in the name of the only begotten Son of God."

Salvation is so simple.

- Salvation is your contract with Jesus (*There is a time, at the end of the age, when Jesus will be Judge and will find each of our destinations, whether heaven or hell).*

- *Make sure you read the small print (Romans 1:20:* "For the invisible things of him from the creation of the world are seen, being understood by the things that made, even his eternal power and Godhead; so that they are without excuse:")

"Romans 1:20 "For the invisible things of him from the creation of the world are seen, being understood by the things that are made, even his eternal power and Godhead; so that they are without excuse:"

"Invisible things": Or attributes, referring specifically to the two mentioned in this verse.

"The things that made": The creation delivers a clear, unmistakable message about God's person.

"His eternal power": The Creator, who made all that we see around us and constantly sustains it, must be a being of incredible power.

They are without excuse:"

God holds all men responsible for their refusal to acknowledge what He has shown them of Himself in His creation. Even those who have never had an opportunity to hear the gospel have received a clear witness about the existence and character of God and have suppressed it.

If a person will respond to the revelation he has, even if it is solely natural revelation, God will provide some means for that person to hear the gospel. (Acts 8:26-39; 10:1-48; 17:27).

Many do not receive God because they have preconceived ideas of how it is so hard to be saved.

Faith in the name of Jesus Christ, speaking of this belief to others, and a love for God that surpasses all others intertwined that they are inseparable.

To believe in Him wholly and genuinely changes our life.

"To believe in him": means more than mere knowledge of the gospel's claims. It includes trust and commitment to Christ as Lord and Savior, which results in receiving a new nature (verse 7), which produces a change in heart and obedience to the Lord.

Believing in the name of Jesus thus causes us to keep His commandments. To believe in His name brings peace, joy, and hope. If we think, we are assured of the resurrection.

We are not like those who have refused Him and have no hope. When Thomas asked Jesus how he could know the way, *Jesus said, "I am the Way, the Truth, and the Life."*

John 3:19: "And this is the condemnation, that light is come into the world, and men loved darkness rather than light because their deeds were evil."

We have spoken so much about the Light. *The Light is Jesus.* This Light gives everything the power to live. The best thing this Light does is do away with darkness.

The great thing about this Light is that it shines into all the corners of life and makes manifest visible the works.

People who have rejected the Light of Jesus want their deeds to be hidden by darkness. They are ashamed to have them out in the open.

I have said it before but notice that most crimes are done under darkness. Where light is absent, darkness prevails.

Everything about darkness pertains to Satan and his crowd.

Come to the Light and let this Light do away with all the darkness in your life.

John 3:20: "For everyone that do evil hate the light, neither come to the light, lest his deeds should be rebuked."

The evildoer will hate the Light because it would reveal his immoral conduct. It could have to do with the followers of Jesus (Light) and the followers of Satan (darkness).

Those who drink, swear, and do all sorts of nasty things hate those who do good things. It gives the evil children of darkness a terrible guilt compound to be around those of truth and life.

Judgments will come up, and those who walk in darkness will fall short.

Those who are living evil lives hate those who are following Jesus. Their sins make them feel guilty, and that causes them to hate.

John 3:21: "But he that do truth come to the light, that his deeds may be made manifest, that they wrought in God."

Truth, love, joy, peace, honesty, and happiness need no darkness to hide in. They are products of the Light. Those who live in the Light are eager to have any small things that are not pleasing to God become known to them so they can get rid of them.

They are growing constantly in honesty, peace, and truth. The Light reveals what is there. If they are good deeds, you do not want them hidden.

Romans 2:1: "Therefore thou art inexcusable, O man, whosoever thou art that judges: for wherein thou judge another, thou condemn thyself; for thou that judges do the same things."

It is straightforward for us to see sin in other's lives when we often cannot see the same sin in our own lives.

Many ministers have the attitude that they are exempt because they preach. The same law applies to us all.

There are not two sets of rules:

• One for the congregation and one for the preacher. "All have sinned and come short of the glory of God."

• Everyone needs Jesus as Savior and Lord.

Both Jews, Paul's primary audience here, and moral Gentiles who think they are exempt from God's judgment because they have not spoiled in the immoral excesses are tragically mistaken.

They have more knowledge than the immoral pagan and thus a greater accountability.

"Condemn thyself:"

If someone has sufficient knowledge to judge others, he condemns himself because he shows how to evaluate his condition.

Do the same things:"

They have excused and overlooked their sins in condemning others. Self-righteousness exists because of two deadly errors.

- Minimizing God's moral standard, usually by emphasizing externals; and

- Underestimating the depth of one's sinfulness.

Romans 2:2: "But we are sure that the judgment of God is according to truth against them which commit such things."

God will not punish anyone on this evidence. God judges in Truth. He knows what the Truth is even before we begin.

"According to the truth": The meaning is 'right." Whatever God does is right.

Romans 2:3: "And think thou this, O man, that judges them which do such things, and do the same, that thou shalt escape the judgment of God?"

"Condemn thyself:" If someone has sufficient knowledge to judge others, he condemns himself because he shows he can evaluate his condition.

Romans 2:4: "Or despises thou the riches of his goodness and forbearance and longsuffering; not knowing that the goodness of God leadeth thee to repentance?"

"Despises": Meaning to despise or to think down on, thus, to underestimate someone's or something's value, and even to treat with contempt.

"Goodness" refers to "common grace," the benefits God bestows on all men.

"Forbearance": This word, *"to hold back,"* was sometimes used for a truce between warring parties. God graciously holds back His judgment rather than destroying every person the moment they sin.

He saves sinners physically and temporally from what they deserve to show them His saving character so they might come to Him and receive spiritual and eternal salvation.

"Longsuffering" indicates the duration for which God demonstrates His goodness and forbearance for long periods.

Together, these three words speak of God's common grace, the way He demonstrates His grace to all humanity.

"Repentance" is turning from sin to Christ for forgiveness and salvation.

Romans 2:5: "But after thy hardness and impenitent heart treasures up unto thyself wrath against the day of wrath and revelation of the righteous judgment of God;"

The English word "sclerosis" (as in arteriosclerosis, a hardening of the arteries) comes from the Greek word. But here, the danger is not physical but spiritual hardness.

"Impenitent heart": A refusal to repent and accept God's pardon of sin through Jesus and cling to one's wrong is to accumulate more of God's wrath and earn a severe judgment.

"Day of wrath … judgment": Refers to the final judgment of wicked men that comes at the Great White Throne at the end of the Millennium.

Although Scripture everywhere teaches that salvation is not based on works, it consistently teaches that God's judgment is always based on man's deeds.

Paul describes the deeds of four distinct groups:

- The redeemed (verses 7 and 10)

- The unredeemed as shown (verses 8-9).

- The deeds of the redeemed are not the basis of their salvation but the evidence of it.

- They are not perfect and are prone to sin, but there is indisputable evidence of righteousness in their lives.

Romans 2:6 "Who will render to every man according to his deeds:"

We are all storing up things in heaven now. Some who walk in the Light of Jesus store good treasures in heaven.

Matthew 6:19-21 "Lay not up for yourselves treasures upon earth, where moth and rust doth corrupt, and where thieves break through and steal:" "But lay up for yourselves treasures in heaven, where neither moth nor rust doth corrupt, and where thieves do not break through nor steal:" "For where your treasure is, there will your heart be also."

- If our deeds are evil, the wrath of God will be our just payment.

- If we are working for God, only a warm welcome awaits us, and the statement (well done thy good and faithful servant).

- In (verse 7), we see the rewards awaiting the believer.

Romans 2:7 says, "To them who by patient continuance in well doing seek for glory and honor and immortality, eternal life:"

- Even though eternal life is a gift.

- We must continue walking in the salvation Jesus has provided for us.

- We must continue walking in the Light.

- We must be doing the Word and not just hearing the Word.

Verse seven is not simply speaking in duration because even unbelievers will live forever and in worth. Eternal life is a kind of life, the holy life that the everlasting God has given to believers.

We see (verse 8) what awaits those who are not walking with Jesus in His Light.

Romans 2:8: "But unto them that are contentious, and do not obey the truth, but obey unrighteousness, indignation, and wrath,"

God is not unaware. He will punish those who do not obey. From Genesis to Revelation, we see blessings for those who live for God and curses for those who are the children of disobedience.

Romans 2:9-10 "Tribulation and anguish, upon every soul of man that doeth evil, of the Jew first, and also of the Gentile;" "But glory, honor, and peace, to every man that worketh good, to the Jew first, and to the Gentile:"

Just as the Jews are given the first opportunity to hear and respond to the gospel, they will be first to receive God's judgment if they refuse. Israel will receive stricter punishment because she was given more excellent light and blessing.

Romans 2:11: "For there is no respect of persons with God."

God is not impressed with our worldly wealth, importance, position, influence, popularity, or appearance. We are what we are because God chose it to be that way.

If you are jealous of someone's wealth or place in society, blame God. The real reason might be that God could not trust you with wealth or importance. It might even be for your good.

We do not even choose our nationality; God does. We were born and raised in a particular family because God arranged it that way.

Why should anyone be so proud of themselves, this being the case? The only wealth that amounts to anything is what we have stored in heaven.

Romans 2:12: "For as many as have sinned without law shall also perish without law: and as many as have sinned in the law shall be judged by the law;"

"Sinned without law":

The Gentiles who never had the opportunity to know God's moral law will be judged on their disobedience due to their limited knowledge as we studied (1:19-20).

"Sinned in the law":

The Jews and many Gentiles who had access to God's moral law will be accountable for their more excellent knowledge.

To those to whom much is given, much is required.

The Lord is a just God. He judges each according to their knowledge.

Luke 12:48: "But he that knew not, and did commit things worthy of stripes, shall be beaten with few stripes. For unto whomsoever much is given, of him shall be much required: and to whom men have committed much, of him they will ask the more."

If we know to do good and do it not, it is counted sin to us.

3 John 1:11 "Beloved, follow not that which is evil, but that which is good. He that doeth good is of God: but he that doeth evil hath not seen God."

We mentioned before that even nature tells you of God. Our conscience tells us when we are sinning.

We all know right from wrong. The Jews had the law, so they would be judged by their law, if they did not receive Jesus.

All will be judged guilty of sin, who have not accepted complete pardon through Jesus Christ our Lord.

All deserve death. We receive our life in Jesus Christ who is Life.

Romans 2:13 "For not the hearers of the law are just before God, but the doers of the law shall be justified."

Just to hear the law and to do nothing about it would not help at all, and just hearing about Jesus will not save you either. We must act upon what we hear.

The burden is laid on the person receiving salvation to accept it. We have free will which God will not violate.

Romans 10:9-10 "That if thou shalt confess with thy mouth the Lord Jesus, and shalt believe in thine heart that God hath raised him from the dead, thou shalt be saved." "For with the heart, man believeth unto righteousness; and with the mouth, confession is made unto salvation."

Romans 2:14 "For when the Gentiles, which have not the law, do by nature the things contained in the law, these, having not the law, are a law unto themselves:"

Without knowing the written law of God, people in pagan society usually cost and attempt to practice its most basic beliefs.

It is normal for cultures unconsciously to price justice, honesty, compassion, and goodness toward others, reflecting the divine law written in the heart.

"Law unto themselves": Their practice of some good deeds and their hatred of some evil ones show a characteristic knowledge of God's law, a knowledge that will be witnessed against them on the day of judgment.

Romans 2:15 "Which shew the work of the law written in their hearts, their conscience also bearing witness, and their thoughts the mean while accusing or else excusing one another."

"Work of the law": "the same works the Mosaic law prescribes."

"Conscience": with knowledge." That intuitive sense of right and wrong produces guilt when violated.

In addition to a distinctive awareness of God's law, men have a warning system that activates when they choose to ignore or disobey that law.

Paul urges believers not to violate their consciences or cause others to because repeatedly ignoring the conscience's warnings pacifies it and eventually silences it.

Acts 2:38 "Then Peter said unto them, Repent, and be baptized every one of you in the name of Jesus Christ for the remission of sins, and ye shall receive the gift of the Holy Ghost."

"Repent": This refers to a change of mind and purpose that turns an individual from sin to God (1 Thess. 1:9). Such change involves more than fearing the consequences of God's judgment.

Genuine repentance knows that the evil of sin must be forsaken, and the person and work of Christ totally and singularly embraced. Peter exhorted his hearers to repent, otherwise they would not experience true conversion (Matt. 3:2; Acts 3:19; 5:31; 8:22; 11:18; 17:30; 20:21; 26:20; Matt. 4:17).

"Be baptized": means "be dipped or immersed" in water.

Peter was obeying Christ's command from Matt. 28:19 and urging the people who repented and turned to the Lord Christ for salvation to name, through the waters of baptism, with His death, burial, and resurrection (Acts 19:5; Rom. 6:3-4; 1 Cor. 12:13; Gal. 3:27; Matt. 3:2).

It was the first time the apostles publicly enjoined people to obey that ceremony.

Before this, many Jews had experienced the baptism of John the Baptist, (Matt. 3:1-3) and were also familiar with the baptism of Gentile converts to Christians.

"In the name of Jesus Christ":

For the new believer, it was a crucial but costly identification to accept.

"For the remission of sins": "because of the forgiveness of sins". Baptism does not produce forgiveness and cleansing from sin. (1 Pet. 3:20-21.

The genuineness of forgiveness goes before the ceremony of baptism (verse 41).

Genuine repentance brings from God the forgiveness of sins (Eph. 1:7), and because of that the new believer was to be baptized.

Baptism: however, was to be the ever-present act of obedience, so that it became synonymous with salvation. Thus, to say one was baptized for forgiveness was the same as saying one was saved, one baptism" in Eph. 4:5.

Every believer enjoys the complete forgiveness of sins (Matt. 26:28; Luke 24:47; Eph. 1:7; Col. 2:13; 1 John 2:12).

"The gift of the Holy Ghost": 1:5, 8.

Here, as throughout Scripture, one aspect of conversion is commonly used to stand for all aspects:

Believing and calling as well as repenting. The correct name for allowing part of something to stand for the whole is called synecdoche.

Repentance is something every person must do (17:30). For several reasons *"be baptized"* should not be joined with *"for the remission of sins"* to teach baptismal revival.

First, the situation of this route shows that only repentance is linked with the removal of sin at salvation:

"Whosoever shall call ... shall be saved" (verse 21).

• "Repent ... that your sins may be blotted out" (3:19).

• Second, men prove their faith and salvation before baptism (10:43-47). You must believe in your heart the Lord Jesus and confess with your mouth you should be saved. You must believe in the Holy Ghost to receive it.

• Third, do include water baptism in the salvation experience – John 3:16; Acts 16:31; Romans 4:10; Eph. 2:1-10; 1 Pet. 1:18-19.

"Repent for the remission of sins, and you will receive the gift, which is the Holy Spirit, and let each of you be baptized in the name of Christ."

Though water baptism does not save or wash away our sins, it is a command that needs to be obeyed speedily after conversion.

Jesus commanded it (Matt. 28:19-20), as does Peter here. It is the consistent pattern throughout Acts (16:31-34; 18:8).

These men Peter was speaking to here were the house of Israel. They had rejected Jesus as their Messiah. They must repent of this rejection of Jesus as the substitute for their sin.

The one they had rejected is the very one they are to be baptized in the name of. These are all Jews here. They must repent of rejecting Jesus. They had the law; the Gentiles did not have the law to go by.

The gift of the Holy Ghost would come after they had repented and been baptized. The part of those who want to be saved is to repent of their sin, and then believe in the name of Jesus Christ.

Just as Abraham was justified just as if he had never sinned by faith they will be justified by faith in Jesus Christ. God will save all who call on His name.

Acts 2:39 "For the promise is unto you, and to your children, and to all that are afar off, even as many as the Lord our God shall call."

*The promise is made to whosoever will. (1:*4).

"All that are afar off": Gentiles, who would also share in the blessings of salvation (Eph. 2:11-13). Gentiles of all generations since the Jews are thought of as those who are nearby.

The Lord Jesus died for all, but we must accept the gift of salvation. God calls all of us, but few accept that call.

"As many as the Lord our God shall call": Salvation is ultimately from the Lord. (Rom. 3:24).

Acts 2:40 "And with many other words did he testify and exhort, saying, Save yourselves from this unfortunate generation".

"Unfortunate" means "morally crooked" or "perverse."

We see that this group that Peter is speaking to is the very group that turned Jesus down. This says that Peter kept on speaking to them to make them understand their need for Jesus as Savior.

Romans 6:20 "For when ye were the servants of sin, ye were free from righteousness."

Paul is explaining here, and he is making this just as clear as he can so that they will understand. He is not just speaking in parables or even spiritually, but exactly so those in the flesh can understand. Sin occurs through lust of the flesh.

"Ye were free from righteousness": Meaning spiritually dead in sins and trespasses.

Romans 6:21 "What fruit had ye then in those things whereof ye are now ashamed? for the end of those things is death."

James 1:15 "Then when lust hath conceived, it bringeth forth sin: and sin, when it is finished, bringeth forth death."

In Corinthians, some of the fruit of unrighteousness will keep a person from inheriting the kingdom of God.

1 Corinthians 6:9-10 "Know ye not that the unrighteous shall not inherit the kingdom of God? Be not deceived: neither fornicators, nor idolaters, nor adulterers, nor effeminate, nor abusers of themselves with mankind," "Nor thieves, nor covetous, nor drunkards, nor revilers, nor extortioners, shall inherit the kingdom of God."

Romans 6:22 "But now being made free from sin, and become servants to God, ye have your fruit unto holiness, and the end everlasting life."

A servant obeys his master. Obedience is better than sacrifice (1 Samuel 15:22). God wants our loyalty and our love.

Ephesians 5:9 "For the fruit of the Spirit is in all goodness and righteousness and truth."

All of this is saying to us, that if Jesus is living inside of us, we will walk through this life as if Jesus was taking the steps Himself.

Self will be no more; Christ-in-me shall rule. If we do not give up, we will inherit eternal life.

Galatians 6:9 "And let us not be weary in well doing: for in due season, we shall reap if we faint not."

"Holiness":

The benefit of being slaves to God is sanctification, the outcome of which is eternal life.

Romans 6:23 "For the wages of sin is death, but the gift of God is eternal life through Jesus Christ our Lord."

Describes two unavoidable absolutes:

- Spiritual death is the paycheck for every man's slavery to sin, a

- Eternal life is a gift God gives undeserving sinners who believe in His Son.

We are in the last days of a time when:

- violence,

- murder,

- homosexuality,

- sexual immorality,

- human trafficking,

- sodomite,

- false teaching.

When evil and uncertainty are very much in our sight and growing daily.

The world is looking for answers and some Christians are looking for encouragement to know who God is and strengthen their faith in the Lord.

Many Christians and unsaved humanity don't know about the book of Revelation and its purpose in the greater scheme of things that is happening.

In my books, I draw upon years of biblical study and research to shed some light on a subject that is close and dear to the Lord's heart for souls.

We can see in the Book of Revelation many warnings throughout the book, there are many movies about the history and stories of the Seven Churches.

What about the warnings and danger of the sins and no repentance of humanity in these churches and where their destination will be?

- *The Lamb Book of Life* for the saved

- The Book of damnation for the unsaved.

There is no longer A Fear of God!

And do not fear those who kill the body but cannot kill the soul. But rather fear him (Jesus) who can destroy both soul and body in hell. (Matthew 10: 28).

The road to Hell is paved with the bones of priests and monks, and the skulls of Bishops are the lamp posts that light the path.

Chapter 6

Free From Indwelling Sin

Romans 8:1 "There is therefore now no condemnation to them which are in Christ Jesus, who walk not after the flesh, but after the Spirit."

So many Christians want to stop with the statement "There is therefore now no condemnation to them which are in Christ Jesus". This statement is true only if the last part of this statement is kept. Salvation is a daily walk.

There is no condemnation in righteousness. If we walk in righteousness, not after the flesh but after the Spirit of God there is no condemnation. To preach that Christians are above condemnation when they are living like the world is in error. If you are walking in the Spirit of God, there is nothing to condemn you for.

The word condemnation is used only three times in the New Testament and only in the book of Romans.

"*Condemnation*" refers to a verdict of guilty and the penalty that the verdict demands. No sin a true believer commits whether past, present, or future can be held against him since the penalty was paid by Christ and righteousness was imputed to the believer.

Romans 8:2 "For the law of the Spirit of life in Christ Jesus hath made me free from the law of sin and death."

The word "For" introduces the reason there is no condemnation for the believer; the Spirit has replaced the law with the Old Testament law. Although it is good, holy, and righteous, because of the weakness of the flesh, no one can keep it.

The old law, which was God's commandments, showed men how they should live, but that law because of the weakness of the flesh could only produce sin and death as it could not save.

This is shown in (Romans 3:23), which tells us all have sinned and come short of the glory of God. And again in (Romans 6:23), which clearly says that the wages of sin is death.

The new, simple law of grace produces life, the law of faith, or the message of the gospel.

Romans 8:3 "For what the law could not do, in that it was weak through the flesh, God sending his own Son in the likeness of sinful flesh, and for sin, condemned sin in the flesh:"

"What the law could not do" was it could not deliver sinners from its penalty.

Because of the sinful corruption of unregenerate men, the law was powerless to produce righteousness.

In Christ's incarnation when He became fully man, He took only the outward appearance of sinful flesh, but He was completely without sin.

God's condemnation against sin was fully poured out on the sinless flesh of Christ.

Romans 8:4 "That the righteousness of the law might be fulfilled in us, who walk not after the flesh, but after the Spirit."

We see from this Scripture above, that it is possible to walk in the Spirit of God and not fulfill the desires of the flesh.

This is a state of being for all true Christians who have turned over their free will to the perfect will of God.

We, like Jesus, must come to a place where we can say not my will be done, but thine oh Lord.

"The righteousness of the law" refers to the thoughts, words, and deeds that the moral law of God demands. It finds its basis in the character of God and is presented in outline form in the Ten Commandments.

Its most condensed form is in Jesus' commands to love God and to love one's neighbor as oneself.

Although the believer is no longer in bondage to the moral law's condemnation and penalty as we studied last (chapter 7:6), the law still reflects the moral character of God and His will for His creatures.

A believer's walk refers to their lifestyle and the habits of living and thinking that characterize a person's life.

Then since every true Christian is indwelt by the Spirit, every Christian will manifest the fruit He (referring to God), produces in his life.

Romans 8:5 "For they that are after the flesh do mind the things of the flesh; but they that are after the Spirit the things of the Spirit."

We cannot be fleshing man and spirit man both. One spirit will rule. In other words, we cannot keep one foot in the world and one foot in heaven.

When it speaks of *"the flesh", this is referring to unbelievers*.

Here this is speaking of a basic orientation of the mind. A mindset that includes one's affections, mental processes, and will.

Paul's point here is that unbelievers' basic disposition is to satisfy the cravings of their unredeemed flesh.

When scripture speaks of "they that are after the Spirit" is simply speaking of believers.

Romans 8:6 "For to be carnally minded is death; but to be spiritually minded is life and peace."

Carnally means "of flesh". This is a simple spiritual equation: The person with the mind set on the flesh is spiritually dead.

But to be spiritually minded is describing every Christian. The person with his mind set on the things of the Spirit is very much spiritually alive and at peace with God.

Galatians 6:8 "For he that soweth to his flesh shall of the flesh reap corruption; but he that soweth to the Spirit shall of the Spirit reap life everlasting."

This is just one more way to say that our flesh desires to sin and our spirit desires to please God.

Romans 8:7 "Because the carnal mind is enmity against God: for it is not subject to the law of God, neither indeed can be."

This very statement is why mind control is so bad. The mind, not given over to the Lord Jesus Christ, truly can have power, but it is from the wrong source.

Mind power tells us that we have the power within ourselves to bring miracles about. It is saying we don't need God; we can do it ourselves.

The unbeliever's problem is much deeper than acts of disobedience, which are merely outward manifestations of inner fleshly compulsions.

His basic inclinations and orientation toward gratifying himself, however outwardly religious or moral he may appear, are directly hostile to God.

Even the good deeds unbelievers perform are not truly a fulfillment of God's law, because they are produced by the flesh, for selfish reasons, and from a heart that is in rebellion.

Romans 8:8 "So then they that are in the flesh cannot please God."

The flesh desires things of this earth, but the spirit is stayed upon God's will in our lives. Read (1 Corinthians 15:35), to understand about the spirit man who lives when the flesh dies.

The flesh and its desires must die so that the spirit man can live.

Romans 8:9 "But ye are not in the flesh, but in the Spirit, if so be that the Spirit of God dwell in you. Now if any man has not the Spirit of Christ, he is none of his."

"Dwell" refers to being in one's own home. The Spirit of God makes His home in every person who trusts in Jesus Christ.

When there is no evidence of His presence by the fruit He produces through us, a person has no legitimate claim to Christ as Savior and Lord.

Galatians 2:20 says it all. "I am crucified with Christ: nevertheless, I live; yet not I, but Christ live in me: and the life which I now live in the flesh I live by the faith of the Son of God, who loved me, and gave himself for me."

Romans 8:10 "And if Christ be in you, the body is dead because of sin; but the Spirit is life because of righteousness."

This body referred to is actually "our old man".

Our old self died with Christ, and the life we now enjoy is a new divinely given life that is the life of Christ Himself.

We have been removed from the unregenerate self's presence and control, so we should not follow the remaining memories of its old sinful ways as if we were still under its evil influence.

It is best to translate the word "*spirit*" as the person's spirit, not the Holy Spirit. Paul is saying that if God's Spirit indwells you as we discussed (in verse 9), the human spirit is alive and can manifest true righteousness.

Romans 8:11 But if the Spirit of him that raised Jesus from the dead dwell in you, he that raised Christ from the dead shall also quicken your mortal bodies by his Spirit that dwelleth in you.

As a believer, the same Spirit dwells in you. God's Holy Spirit raised Christ from the dead and it is the same Spirit who will quicken the believers and shall also resurrect us too.

Chapter 7

Sonship Through the Spirit

Romans 8:12 "Therefore, brethren, we are debtors, not to the flesh, to live after the flesh."

Our old flesh died with Christ and the life we now enjoy is a new divinely given life that is the life of Christ Himself. We have been removed from the unregenerate self's presence and control, so we should not follow the remaining memories of its old sinful ways as if we were still under its evil influence.

Therefore, we are debtors, not to the flesh, which is our old selves, but to the Spirit of Christ as we saw (verse 9).

You see we do not owe our bodies anything. The flesh is our enemy. If we obey the lust of the flesh, we are living in sin. We must overcome the flesh and put it in subjection to the spirit.

Romans 8:13 "For if ye live after the flesh, ye shall die but if ye through the Spirit do mortify the deeds of the body, ye shall live."

Here again, we see the warfare that goes on within each of us. Our spirit wants to do the things of God and our flesh lusts for the things of the flesh and the world. If we choose to let the Spirit of God rule our life, and in so doing "kill the flesh" we shall live for all of eternity in heaven with Jesus. If we choose to follow the ways of the world, it brings eternal damnation and total separation from God.

Paul's instruction is what to do in the struggle with sin in this verse, then destroys several false views of how believers are made holy:

- That in a crisis moment we are at once made perfect.

- That we must "let God" take over while we still are idle.

- That some turning point decision will propel us to a higher level of holiness.

Instead, Paul tells us that the Spirit provides us with the energy and power to continually and gradually be killing our sins, a process never completed in this life.

The means the Spirit uses to do this process is our faithful obedience to the simple commands of Scripture.

<u>Romans 8:14 "For as many as are led by the Spirit of God, they are the sons of God."</u>

Scripture does not teach us that we are led through subjective, mental impressions or promptings to provide direction in making life's decisions. Instead, God's Spirit objectively leads His children sometimes through the orchestration of circumstances by:

- Illumination, divinely clarifying Scripture to make it understandable to our sinful, finite minds.

- Sanctification, divinely enabling us to obey Scripture.

- When a person experiences the Spirit's leading in those ways, he gains assurance that God has adopted him into His family.

- That Spirit within us makes us God's children.

<u>*Galatians 3:26 "For ye are all the children of God by faith in Christ Jesus."*</u>

<u>*Romans 8:15 "For ye have not received the spirit of bondage again to fear; but ye have received the Spirit of adoption, whereby we cry, Abba, Father."*</u>

Unregenerate people are slaves to their fear of death because of their life of sin, and to fear their final punishment.

<u>*A very similar Scripture is in 1 Corinthians.*</u>

1 Corinthians 2:12 "Now we have received, not the spirit of the world, but the spirit which is of God; that we might know the things that are freely given to us of God."

The *"Spirit of adoption"* isn't a reference to the transaction by which God adopts us, but to a Spirit-produced awareness of the rich reality that God has made us His children, therefore we can come before Him without fear or hesitation as our beloved Father.

When God adopted us into his family, then that made us heirs to all he owns. We will be joint heirs with Jesus as we read (in verse 17 of Romans 8).

There are three places in the New Testament where Abba is used; one here (Romans 8:15); one (Mark 14:36), and one (Galatians 4:6).

Mark 14:36 "And he said, Abba, Father, all things are possible unto thee; take away this cup from me: nevertheless, not what I will, but what thou wilt."

Galatians 4:6 "And because ye are sons, God hath sent forth the Spirit of his Son into your hearts, crying, Abba, Father."

We see in all these three verses, that this name is reserved for only the children of God to call Him by meaning Daddy or Papa and brings tenderness, dependence, and a relationship free of fear or anxiety.

Romans 8:16 "The Spirit itself bear witness with our spirit, that we are the children of God:"

In Roman culture, for an adoption to be legally binding, seven reputable witnesses had to be present, attesting to its validity.

God's Holy Spirit confirms the validity of our adoption, not by some inner, mystical voice, but by the fruit He produces in us and the power He provides for spiritual service.

The first Spirit in the sentence above is Capitalized meaning the Holy Spirit of God (or the Spirit of the risen Christ).

This Spirit within us is God's Spirit. There is plenty of evidence in our lives when this Spirit dwells within us because we allow Christ to live through our actions and deeds. We become Christ-like.

Romans 8:17 "And if children, then heirs; heirs of God, and joint heirs with Christ; if so be that we suffer with him, that we may be also glorified together."

If you are a believer, you are an heir of God. We will then inherit eternal salvation, God Himself, glory, and everything in the universe.

Unlike the Jewish practice of the primacy of the firstborn son, under Roman law, the inheritance was divided equally between the children, where the law more carefully protected possessions that had been inherited.

"Joint heirs": God has appointed His Son to be heir of all things. Every adopted child will receive by divine grace the full inheritance Christ receives by divine right.

"Suffer with Him" is proof of the believer's ultimate glory in that he suffers, whether it comes as mockery, ridicule, or physical persecution, because of his Lord.

Chapter 8

From Suffering to Glory

Romans 8:18 "For I reckon that the sufferings of this present time are not worthy to be compared with the glory which shall be revealed in us."

In short, this describes the trials and tribulations that we go through in this life on earth. Paul puts this clearly (in 2 Cor. 4:17)

When he says: *"For our light affliction*, which is but for a moment, worketh for us a far more exceeding and eternal weight of glory".

Paul's testimony lists a seemingly unbearable litany of sufferings and persecutions he endured throughout his life, yet he viewed them as weightless and lasting for only a moment.

To Paul, the future glory he would experience with the Lord far outweighed any suffering he experienced in this world. *Paul understood that the greater the suffering, the greater would be his eternal glory.*

Paul can speak first-hand about suffering. He was stoned, shipwrecked, and so many times left for dead: suffering was no stranger to him.

*"Glory": L*ooks forward to the resurrection of the body and the subsequent complete Christlikeness which is the believer's eternal glory.

We can easily see that this present suffering is minor compared to the great glory we will receive when Jesus recognizes us as His when we stand before Him in heaven.

Romans 8:19 "For the earnest expectation of the creature wait for the manifestation of the sons of God."

The creature or creation eagerly looks forward to the revelation of the sons of God in the Millennium the 1000-year earthly reign, because that is the time when the curse will be lifted, and creation will be restored to Edenic conditions.

Everyone who believes in Jesus Christ is also earnestly awaiting the coming of Christ and our eternal life as a son of God.

While we are in a fleshly body, it is our most blessed hope. When we leave this body and are in heaven with Jesus, it will be a reality.

Romans 8:20-21 "For the creature was made subject to vanity, not willingly, but because of him who hath subjected the same in hope," "Because the creature itself also shall be delivered from the bondage of corruption into the glorious liberty of the children of God."

Vanity has several meanings. *Futility, emptiness, frailty, and folly* are all references to the curse of Genesis and consider the whole thing as unnecessary. Creation did not actively participate in the Fall.

It refers to the inability to achieve a goal or purpose. Because of man's sin, God cursed the physical universe and now, no part of creation entirely fulfills God's original purpose.

"Delivered from the bondage of corruption":

There will be no more death. The creature or creation looks forward to the Millennium when the redeemed man is glorified and will never again have to face God's curse.

Romans 8:22 "For we know that the whole creation groan and travailed in pain together until now."

"Groaned and travailed in pain" refers to Adam's Fall, which has caused misery from then until the present. The present sufferings of creation are the "birth pangs" of the new age to be born, the Millennium. From the Fall until now, creation has been groaning over the pointlessness of having been made subject to a curse.

It eagerly looks forward to the time when the curse will be lifted.

Until Jesus' sacrificial death on the cross, there was no promise of everlasting life.

Mankind can die with no hope of everlasting life.

The _atonement_: payment, for sins up until Jesus' crucifixion, was just for one year at a time. The blood of an animal could not do away with sin, it could only cover it.

Romans 8:23 "And not only they, but ourselves also, which have the first fruits of the Spirit, even we groan within ourselves, waiting for the adoption, to wit, the redemption of our body."

- The Holy Spirit is the first installment of the glory yet to follow.

- In the first chapter of James, we read of the Christians being first fruits.

James 1:18 "Of his will begat he us with the word of truth, that we should be a kind of first fruits of his creatures."

1 Corinthians 15:23 "But every man in his order: Christ the first fruits; afterward they that are Christ's at his coming."

This is speaking of those who received the baptism of the Holy Ghost at Pentecost. Receiving the Spirit of God inside of you is a first fruit promise of the resurrection.

Definition of Pentecost:

(Greek _Pentecost, "fiftieth day"_).

Christian festival commemorating the descent of the Holy Spirit on the disciples of Jesus, occurring on the Jewish Pentecost, after Jesus' death, resurrection, and ascension.

The disciples began to speak in the many languages of the people assembled there, a sign that the disciples should spread the Christian message throughout the world.

Jewish Pentecost was a thanksgiving feast for the first fruits of the wheat harvest and was associated with the remembrance of God's gift of the Law to Moses on Mount Sinai. Christian Pentecost is celebrated on the Sunday concluding the fifty days following Easter.

It is also the name of the Jewish celebration of Shavuot (*"Festival of Weeks"*).

The believer groans because of the conflict experienced (7:14-24), from which he needs a final and complete deliverance.

It is the ultimate answer to (7:24). "***O wretched man that I am! Who shall deliver me from the body of this death?***"

Christ will deliver us by the resurrection and glorification of our bodies. Not the physical body only, but all of man's remaining fallenness.

Romans 8:24-25 "For we are saved by hope: but hope that is seen is not hope: for what a man sees, why doth he yet hope for?" "But if we hope for that we see not, then do we with patience wait for it."

Unlike the English *word "hope,"* the New Testament word contains no uncertainty. It speaks of something certain, but not yet realized.

The believer's ultimate destiny is to share in the very glory of God and that hope will be realized because Christ Himself secures it.

Without the clear and certain promises of the Word of God, the believer would have no basis for hope.

Romans 8:26 "Likewise the Spirit also helped our infirmities: for we know not what we should pray for as we ought: but the Spirit itself maketh intercession for us with groanings which cannot be uttered."

We see the problem that many Christians face when they are praying for others. We all pray to the very best of our ability, and still, we do not always know what to pray for, or how to pray for a particular thing.

This is when the Spirit takes over for us and prays for us. God's Spirit knows exactly what the needs are.

The Spirit also groans along with creation and the believer.

The reference is to the Spirit's interpretation of the believer's innermost feelings, which cannot be put into words as the Spirit knows what's in the heart of man.

Romans 8:27 "And he that searched the hearts know what the mind of the Spirit is, because he maketh intercession for the saints according to the will of God."

This is speaking of the Spirit of God the Holy Spirit, praying for the saints. The Spirit of God knows the will of God. He prays for us "according to" God's will. God knows the desires of our hearts, even before we pray.

No words are necessary because the Father understands and agrees with what the Spirit thinks.

Jude 1:20 "But ye, beloved, building up yourselves on your most holy faith, praying in the Holy Ghost,"

Romans 8:28 "And we know that all things work together for good to them that love God, to them who are the called according to his purpose."

It is another Scripture that is many times misunderstood because most people stop reading when it says, *"to them that love God"*. It truly says much more than that though.

Are we fulfilling God's purpose in our lives? If you are, then all things work together for good to you. The key is "them that are called according to His purpose".

People in all types of ministries forget that God has called them to a particular ministry, and they hurry to get into something of their choosing.

The ministry that God will bless you in is the one He called you to. Sometimes we do not realize exactly what God would have us do.

If we get alone with God and pray and ask Him, He will reveal unto us what He would have us to do.

"To them that love God", is the human perspective.

God is working all things together for good, but those who love God are best able to appreciate that fact because they love Him no matter what. *"To them who are called"* is the divine perspective. Scripture often refers to believers as *"the called"* or *"the elect".*

Romans 8:29 "For whom he did foreknow, he also did predestinate to be conformed to the image of his Son, that he might be the firstborn among many brethren."

"Foreknow" is God's determination from eternity to bring certain ones into a special relationship with Himself.

It is not simple advanced knowledge. This knowledge should also not be understood in the sense of *"being acquainted with,"* but in the sense of *"bringing* into a special relation with".

Foreknowledge is God's determination from eternity to bring certain ones into a special relationship with Himself.

"Predestinate" literally means "to mark off or choose before."

God chooses those He knows will participate in His plan of salvation and extends it to all who respond in faith. The doctrine of predestination in Scripture relates to the foreknowledge of God.

Eph. 1:5: "Having predestinated us unto the adoption of children by Jesus Christ to himself, according to the good pleasure of his will".

Predestination is especially noticeable in the conversion of the apostle Paul. Since he was a blasphemer and persecutor of the church, some Christians had a difficult time believing Paul could be saved even after he so testified.

Still, knowing what Paul was ahead and how would respond, God chose him as Apostle to the Gentiles.

When we understand that God has chosen and predestined us, we should also realize we have been ordained to do good works, to bear fruit, and to become like Jesus.

We see from this scripture, that this predestination did not overrule our will. What this is saying, is that God knew even before you were born, how you would choose.

God has foreknowledge of all happenings, not only in my life and yours, but he knows everything from the beginning of time to the end of time.

This is because of His foreknowledge. It is predestined because He foreknew your decision. Jesus' crucifixion was planned from the foundation of the earth. Jesus is the Son of God.

Jesus paid for you and me to be adopted into the family with His precious blood at Calvary. We are part of the family of God, because our elder brother (God's only begotten Son), purchased our right to be called God's sons.

Romans 8:30 "Moreover whom he did predestinate, them he also called: and whom he called, them he also justified: and whom he justified, them he also glorified."

In 2 Timothy 1:9, we read:

2 Timothy 1:9 "Who hath saved us, and called us with a holy calling, not according to our works, but according to his purpose and grace, which was given us in Christ Jesus before the world began,"

"Called":

The calling (of 8:28), is pre-temporal; it occurred before the creation of the world (Eph. 1:4).

The calling here is temporal and refers to the effectual communication of the gospel, resulting in salvation.

"Justified" indicates being declared righteous. It signifies the believer's judicial standing before God. There is no just cause in man to warrant justification.

It is unmerited favor is bestowed through the redemption paid by Jesus Christ on the cross. The redeemed sinner is released based on the ransom's having been paid, by the Lord.

"Glorified":

Glorification is God's doing.

While God's foreknowledge and predestination take place in eternity, and while God's calling and justification are realized in history, God's glorification is yet future.

It is as certain, however, as the previous works. Hence glorified is in the past tense. From God's point of view, it is already accomplished.

The plan was set at the foundation of the world. Man could not be saved by his deeds; he must have a Savior.

That Savior must have been Jesus Christ our Lord. We do know that God's call for many of His ministers was a call before they were even born, like John the Baptist.

John the Baptist's entire life even before birth was planned by God.

Read the account of John the Baptist's birth (Luke 1). This does not mean that John had no choice. He could have refused, but he didn't.

God knew he would carry out God's purpose in his life. Obedience to God's will in our lives will bring peace in our lives too.

Most people today take their call to serve God far too lightly. It is serious business to answer God's call and serve God.

We must first be able to say, *"Not my will be done, but thine O Lord"* and then say, *"Here am I Lord, send me"*.

Chapter 9

Gods Everlasting Love

Romans 8:31 "What shall we then say to these things? If God be for us, who can be against us?"

The Greek construction is better translated as "Since God is for us."

We read (1 Corinthians):

<u>1 Corinthians 8:12 "But when ye sin so against the brethren, and wound their weak conscience, ye sin against Christ."</u>

God fights for us and gives us the victory. God causes even our enemies to live at peace with us if we are Christians. Those who are opposed to God's people are opposed to God.

<u>*Romans 8:32 "He that spared not his own Son, but delivered him up for us all, how shall he not with him also freely give us all things?"*</u>

The hardest thing for the carnal mind to understand is why God would sacrifice His Son for a bunch of sinners.

We read in Romans Chapter 5:

Romans Chapter 5:8 "But God commended his love toward us, in that, while we were yet sinners, Christ died for us."

Paul's point was, would God do less for His children than He did for His enemies?

The amazing thing is that God loves the worst sinner. God provided through His Son a way out for all. Jesus died for all sin. The way out is through the death and resurrection of Jesus Christ.

The problem is that many will not accept this way out and therefore will die in their sin. The beautiful story in Genesis in the O.T. of Abraham about to sacrifice of his son Isaac is a type and shadow of God sacrificing His Son for all of mankind.

A type or shadow is not exact in every detail but makes you think of the happening it is shadowing. Both Abraham and God were about to sacrifice the one who meant the very most to them. In the case of Abraham, God stopped him and gave him a substitute.

In God's case, there was no one greater than Himself to stop him.

Jesus Christ the only begotten of the Father, was the substitute for all mankind. The greatest gift of love in all time was God loving us enough to give His Son to save us. We deserved to die on that cross, but God the Son took our place for us. He was our substitute.

We read earlier in *Romans 6:23 "For the wages of sin is death, but the gift of God is eternal life through Jesus Christ our Lord."*

1 Corinthians chapter 15:45 "And so it is written, the first man Adam was made a living soul; the last Adam was made a quickening spirit."

God has given us life in Jesus Christ. What more can we ask?

Romans 8:33 "Who shall lay anything to the charge of God's elect? It is God that justified."

No charge is admissible, because the father justifies, in that the son died, was raised, and now intercedes for us. Who can successfully accuse someone whom God has declared righteous?

Some young children learned the hard way not to insult God's elect (2 Kings 2:23-24). They had made fun of Elisha's bald head. Elisha cursed them in the name of the Lord and 42 of them were torn off she bears. It is a very dangerous thing to say bad things about God's elect.

Another example of how God will not allow this is when Miriam spoke against Moses and became leprous. She was cleansed when Moses prayed for her (Numbers 12:10).

These two instances remind us not to come against God's elect. God fights their battles for them. We who are God's are not justified by our deeds, but we are justified because we have been cleansed by the shed blood of Jesus Christ. We are justified because we have taken on the righteousness of Christ.

Romans 8:34 "Who is he that condemned? It is Christ that died, yea rather, that is risen again, who is even at the right hand of God, who also maketh intercession for us."

There are four reasons the believer can never be found guilty. Take note of what verse 34 says as it gets into real specifics.

- Christ died for our sins.

- He rose again.

- He sits at the right hand of the Father.

- He is constantly reminding God that He died to pay the cost for our sins (intercessor).

Hebrews 7:24-25 "But this man, because he continued ever, hath an unchangeable priesthood." "Wherefore he is able also to save them to the uttermost that come unto God by him, seeing he ever live to make intercession for them."

Romans 8:35 "Who shall separate us from the love of Christ? shall tribulation, or distress, or persecution, or famine, or nakedness, or peril, or sword?"

This list of experiences that can't separate the believer from God's love in Christ was not just theory to Paul. It was rather personal testimony from one who had personally survived assaults from these entities and emerged triumphant.

This scripture isn't speaking of our love for Christ, but His love for us which He demonstrated in our salvation.

"Persecution" is indicative of suffering that is inflicted upon us by mankind because of our relationship with Christ.

The scripture asks a very interesting question. In the parable of the Sower (Matthew 13:3), we read about how different people were affected by the cares of the world and turned aside from the love of God. One did not understand the Word (love), he had received, and the evil one immediately took it away.

(Matthew 13:21), we read of another who was slightly stronger than the one mentioned, but in the face of tribulation and persecution lost out.

(Matthew 13:22), tells of someone who cares of the world and the deceitfulness of riches causes them to fail.

Out of all the seed, word or love sown, there was one who received it, and nothing or no one could take it away. This person was not only "not shaken" by all the problems that came but went out and brought others to the Lord.

Problems did not stop this person; it just made him stronger and more determined to do the will of God.

Romans 8:36 "As it is written, for thy sake we are killed all day long; we are accounted as sheep for the slaughter."

Since Jesus was crucified, there have been men and women who were willing to be martyred (killed), to bring the true message of God. Paul in writing this could be speaking of himself.

He was stoned, ship-wrecked, beaten, and left for dead, but he never gave up the cause of Jesus Christ. We are sheep if we are followers of Jesus Christ (the great Shepherd). The sheep will follow the Shepherd even to the death of his body.

Psalm 44:22 "Yea, for thy sake are we killed all day long; we are counted as sheep for the slaughter."

Romans 8:37 "Nay, in all these things we are more than conquerors through him that loved us."

"More than conquerors" is a compound Greek word, which means to over conquer, to conquer completely without any real threat to personal life or health.

A true follower of Jesus Christ will not turn back from those problems listed (verse 35). We know that Jesus has won the victory. These little battles are nothing. Jesus won the war at Calvary. Our strength is in Jesus.

Romans 8:38 "For I am persuaded, that neither death, nor life, nor angels, nor principalities, nor powers, nor things present, nor things to come,"

Principalities are fallen angels or demons. Powers: the plural form of this common word for "power" is used to refer to either miracles or to persons in positions of authority.

Romans 8:39 "Nor height, nor depth, nor any other creature, shall be able to separate us from the love of God, which is in Christ Jesus our Lord."

We cannot be separated from God's love, because it is outlined in a person who is God Himself, Jesus Christ our Savior. God's desire to redeem believers cannot be frustrated, because He is infinitely greater than any potential enemy. His plan will be realized because it is His purpose.

I think the book of (Ephesians 2:18-22), says it all.

"For through him, we both have access by one Spirit unto the Father." "Now therefore ye are no more strangers and foreigners, but fellow citizens with the saints, and of the household of God;" "And are built upon the foundation of the apostles and prophets, Jesus Christ himself being the chief cornerstone;"

"In whom all the building fitly framed together growth unto a holy temple in the Lord:" "In whom ye also are builder together for a habitation of God through the Spirit."

Chapter 10

The World Needs the Gospel

Romans 10:1 "Brethren, my heart's desire and prayed to God for Israel is, that they might be saved."

We have been saying over and over in these lessons how important it was to Paul that the Jewish people would accept Jesus as their Savior.

God called Paul to the Gentiles, but he could not help but desire his people to come to Jesus Christ. We see that the Lord Jesus desired them to be saved as well as Paul, but they would not.

Luke 13:34 "O Jerusalem, Jerusalem, which kill the prophets, and stone them that are sent unto thee; how often would I have gathered thy children together, as a hen doth gather her brood under her wings, and ye would not!"

Paul's calling as an apostle to the Gentiles did not diminish his continual entreaties to God for Israel to be saved, or his evangelistic efforts toward Jews.

Romans 10:2 "For I bear them record that they have a zeal of God, but not according to knowledge."

It is so strange to me that the people who were supposed to know the Word of God the best did not truly understand what that Word was saying, and they rejected their promised Messiah.

The Scripture above says that it was for lack of knowledge. Perhaps, it was for lack of understanding what they were reading.

Hosea 4:6 "My people are destroyed for lack of knowledge: because thou hast rejected knowledge, I will also reject thee, that thou shalt be no priest to me: seeing thou hast forgotten the law of thy God, I will also forget thy children."

The Jews indeed had a "zeal of God" which was demonstrated by their legalistic conformity to the law and their fierce opposition to Judaism's opponents.

Romans 10:3 "For they are ignorant of God's righteousness, and going about to establish their righteousness, have not submitted themselves unto the righteousness of God."

"Ignorant of God's righteousness": means they were ignorant both of God's inherent righteousness revealed in the law and the rest of the Old Testament which should have shown the Jews their unrighteousness, and of the righteousness which comes from Him based on faith.

We see from the following Scriptures, the self-righteousness of the scribes and Pharisees and how it displeased God.

Luke 18:9-14 "And he spoke this parable unto certain which trusted in themselves that they were righteous, and despised others:" "Two men went up into the temple to pray; the one a Pharisee, and the other a publican." "The Pharisee stood and prayed thus with himself, God, I thank thee, that I am not as other men are extortioners, unjust, adulterers, or even as this publican."

"I fast twice in the week, I give tithes of all that I possess." "And the publican, standing afar off, would not lift up so much as his eyes unto heaven, but smote upon his breast, saying, God be merciful to me a sinner." "I tell you; this man went down to his house justified [rather] than the other: for everyone that exalted himself shall be abased, and he that humbles himself shall be exalted."

God loves the humble in heart who are looking to Jesus Christ for their righteousness.

"Their righteousness": means their beliefs were based on their conformity to God's law which was often the less demanding standards of their traditions.

Romans 10:4 "For Christ is the end of the law for righteousness to everyone that believeth."

"*For Christ is the end of the law*": although the Greek word translated "*end*" can mean either "*fulfillment*" or "*termination*." This is not a reference to Christ's having perfectly fulfilled the law through His teaching or his sinless life.

Instead, as the second half of the verse shows, Paul means that belief in Christ as Lord and Savior ends the sinner's futile quest for righteousness through his imperfect attempts to save himself by efforts to obey the law.

Matt. 5:17-18 "Think not that I come to destroy the law or the prophets: I do not come to destroy, but to fulfill." "For verily I say unto you, till heaven and earth pass, one jot or one tittle shall in no wise pass from the law, till all be fulfilled."

Romans 10:5 "For Moses described the righteousness, which is of the law, That the man which doeth those things shall live by them."

Leviticus 18:5 "Ye shall therefore keep my statutes, and my judgments: which if a man do, he shall live in them: I am the Lord."

There were hundreds of the Levitical laws that had to be kept righteous in the law. There was no way that a person could even keep up with them, much less keep them. Jesus came and fulfilled them for us so that we might live by the grace of God.

To hope for righteousness based on obedience to the law requires perfect agreement in every detail, which is an utter impossibility.

Verses 6-9: Paul skillfully weaves together quotations from (Deuteronomy 9:4 and 30:10-14), which speak of God's initiative in grace and man's humble obedience to it. He then applies this truth to the gospel of Christ.

Romans 10:6-7 "But the righteousness, which is of faith speak on this wise, say not in thine heart, who shall ascend into heaven? That is, to bring Christ down from above:" "Or, who shall descend into the deep? That is, to bring up Christ again from the dead."

Paul speaks of righteousness based on faith as if it were a person and puts in their mouth a quotation from Deuteronomy. His point is that the righteousness of faith does not require some impossible journey through the universe to find Christ.

Deuteronomy 9:4 "Speak not thou in thine heart, after that the Lord thy God hath cast them out from before thee, saying, for my righteousness, the Lord hath brought me in to possess this land: but for the wickedness of these nations the Lord doth drive them out from before thee."

Deuteronomy 30:11-14 "For this commandment which I command thee this day, it is not hidden from thee, neither is it far off."

"It is not in heaven, that thou shouldest say, who shall go up for us to heaven, and bring it unto us, that we may hear it, and do it" "Neither is it beyond the sea, that thou shouldest say, who shall go over the sea for us, and bring it unto us, that we may hear it, and do it?"

"But the word is very nigh unto thee, in thy mouth, and in thy heart, that thou mayest do it."

Romans 10:8 "But what saith it? The word is nigh thee, even in thy mouth, and in thy heart: that is, the word of faith, which we preach;"

"The word is nigh thee": is quoted from (Deuteronomy 30:14), which was quoted in the previous scripture. The journey of (verses 6 and 7), is unnecessary because God has revealed the way of salvation: it is by faith. The Word of faith is the message of faith and that is the way to God.

Matthew 10:32-33 "Whosoever, therefore, shall confess me before men, he will I confess also before my Father which is in heaven." "But whosoever shall deny me before men, he will I also deny before my Father which is in heaven."

We can see the importance of the things we say from all of this. Faith, we know, is believing in things we cannot see. If you can see something, it takes no faith to believe.

Jesus Himself said, blessed are those who have not seen and yet believed.

John 20:29 "Jesus saith unto him, Thomas, because thou hast seen me, thou hast believed: blessed are they that have not seen, and yet have believed."

Romans 10:9 "That if thou shalt confess with thy mouth the Lord Jesus, and shalt believe in thine heart that God hath raised him from the dead, thou shalt be saved."

This verse does not mean a simple acknowledgment that He is God and the Lord of the universe, since even demons acknowledge that to be true.

This is the deep personal conviction, without reservation, that Jesus is that person's own master or sovereign. This phrase includes *repenting from sin, trusting in Jesus for salvation, and submitting to Him as Lord.*

This is the volitional element of faith.

We studied this in the first chapter which I'll repeat here:

Believeth: To trust, rely on, or have faith in. When used for salvation, this word usually occurs in the present tense *"is believing"* which stresses that faith is not simply a one-time event, but an ongoing condition.

True saving faith is supernatural, a gracious gift of God that He produces in the heart and is the only means by which a person can appropriate true righteousness.

Saving faith consists of three elements.

- *Mental:* the mind understands the gospel and the truth about Christ

- *Emotional:* one embraces the truthfulness of those facts with sorrow over sin and joy over God's mercy and grace

- *Spiritual:* the sinner submits his will to Christ and trusts in Him alone as the only hope of salvation.

Genuine faith always produces authentic obedience.

"God hath raised Him from the dead":

Christ's resurrection was the supreme validation of His ministry. Belief in it is necessary for salvation because it proves that Christ is who He claimed to be and that the Father had accepted His sacrifice in the place of sinners. Without the resurrection, there is no salvation.

This leaves absolutely no doubt at all about what we must do to be saved.

Romans 10:10 "For with the heart man believeth unto righteousness; and with the mouth, confession is made unto salvation."

"Confession is made unto salvation":

One is not saved by his mouth's conversation, meaning many, who by their head knowledge say they are saved but are not, but rather, the mouth testifies willingly by the grace of God in Christ which has been received by faith for those who have been truly saved and their words are coming from their heart.

Confession is a Greek word that means to say the same thing or to agree with someone. The person who confesses Jesus as Lord agrees with the Father's declaration that Jesus is Savior and Lord.

Romans 10:11 "For the scripture saith, whosoever believeth on him shall not be ashamed."

Let me read this scripture from Isaiah and tell me who it is talking about and how it relates to (Rom: 10:11).

Isaiah 28:16 "Therefore thus saith the Lord God, Behold, I lay in Zion for a foundation a stone, a tried stone, a precious cornerstone, a sure foundation: he that believeth shall not make haste."

"Haste" means disturbed.

The Hebrew word is hurry. The Greek Old Testament interprets this Hebrew hasten for *"hurry" in the sense of "put to shame",* furnishing the basis of the New Testament citations of this verse.

Isaiah 49:23 "And kings shall be thy nursing fathers, and their queens thy nursing mothers: they shall bow down to thee with their face toward the earth and lick up the dust of thy feet, and thou shalt know that I am the Lord: for they shall not be ashamed that wait for me."

Of course, this speaks of our Cornerstone, Jesus.

1 Peter 2:6 "Wherefore also it is contained in the scripture, Behold, I lay in Zion a chief cornerstone, elect, precious: and he that believeth on him shall not be confounded."

If you have made Jesus the Lord of your life, you want to tell everybody you see. Christians are the bride of Christ. Have you ever seen a new bride who can keep quiet about her groom?

Zion or Sion are terms that most often designate the Land of Israel and its capital, Jerusalem.

Romans 10:12 "For there is no difference between the Jew and the Greek: for the same Lord over all is rich unto all that call upon him."

"There is no difference".

_A parenthetical comment explaining that God can bestow His righteousness on all who believe, Jew or Gentile, because all men, without distinction, fail miserably to live up to the divine standard.

Romans 10:13 "For whosoever shall call upon the name of the Lord shall be saved."

Paul quotes (Joel 2:32), to further emphasize that salvation is available for people of all nations and races.

This familiar Old Testament expression does not refer to some desperate cry to just any deity but to the one true God as He has revealed Himself. A revelation that now includes recognition of Jesus as Lord and of the One who raised Jesus from the dead.

As chapter nine stressed divine sovereignty in salvation, this passage stresses human responsibility. Scripture does not view these two principles as paradoxical or contradictory but as mutually compatible truths.

"Saved" is speaking of salvation which is the most common biblical expression used to identify the subjective changes in people's lives, when by faith they have received the benefit of Christ's death and resurrection.

The term implies deliverance, safety, preservation, healing, and soundness. It occurs in three phases.

- First, the Christian has been saved from the guilt and penalty of sin.

- Second, the Christian is being saved from the habit and dominion of sin in this life.

- Finally, when the Lord returns, the Christian will be saved from all the physical results of sin and of God's curse on the world.

Chapter 11

The World Rejects the Gospel

Romans 10:14 "How then shall they call on him in whom they have not believed? and how shall they believe in him of whom they have not heard? and how shall they hear without a preacher?"

In presenting the universal proclamation of the gospel, Paul presents the reasons why a universal proclamation is necessary.

- First, because the call must be preceded by faith, and

- Second, because faith must be preceded by hearing.

- This shows that knowledge is essential to belief. Faith must have a binding content.

- Third, because hearing requires a preacher,

- Fourth, because preaching requires being sent.

- The One who sends is God.

- Salvation is completely from God.

Romans 10:15 "And how shall they preach, except they be sent? As it is written, how beautiful are the feet of them that preach the gospel of peace and bring glad tidings of good things!"

Paul's main point in this series of rhetorical questions is that a clear presentation of the gospel message must precede true saving faith. True faith always has content, the revealed Word of God. Salvation comes to those who hear and believe the facts of the gospel.

"How beautiful are the feet" comes from Isaiah.

Isaiah 52:7 "How beautiful upon the mountains are the feet of him that bringeth good tidings, that publish peace; that bringeth good tidings of good, that publish salvation; that saith unto Zion, Thy God reign!"

It is the message of good news that those feet carry that is so welcome.

Romans 10:16 "But they have not all obeyed the gospel. For Isaiah saith, Lord, who hath believed our report?"

The good news is not only a gracious offer but a command to believe and repent. *"Believed our report"* is a scripture quoted from (Isaiah 53:1).

The report Isaiah described was of the substitutionary death of Christ, the good news of the gospel (Isa 53:5).

Romans 10:17 "So then faith cometh by hearing, and hearing by the word of God."

"The Word of God": or better, the word of Christ. The reference is to the oral communication of the gospel. The word translated "report" in verse 16 is translated as "hearing" here. Notice that it is not faith in what is heard, but faith that comes about by what is heard. This is what Paul meant (Rom. 1:16) when he said the gospel "is the power of God unto salvation."

Saving faith is not man doing his part in response to God's having done His part. Saving faith can come about only through the gospel. Salvation is God's work alone. This also shows that there is no other way to be saved but by the obvious gospel of Christ.

Luke 11:28 "But he said, yea rather, blessed are they that hear the word of God, and keep it."

It is the Word of God that is powerful, that convicts us of our sins and sets us on the road to salvation. Look at the next Scripture and see just how powerful this Word is.

Hebrews 4:12 "For the word of God is quick, and powerful, and sharper than any two-edged sword, piercing even to the dividing asunder of soul and spirit, and of the joints and marrow, and is a discerner of the thoughts and intents of the heart."

Romans 10:18 "But I say, have they not heard? Yes verily, their sound went into all the earth, and their words unto the ends of the world."

Paul cited this quotation from the LXX which is the Greek translation of the Hebrew Old Testament's version of (Psalms 19:4), to show that even David understood that God's revelation of Himself has reached the entire earth.

Romans 10:19-20 "But I say, did not Israel know? First Moses saith, I will provoke you to jealousy by them that are no people, and by a foolish nation I will anger you." "But Isaiah is very bold, and saith, I was found of them that sought me not; I was made manifest unto them that asked not after me."

Israel was ignorant of the salvation truth: contained in their Scriptures, including that the gospel would reach the Gentiles (Deut. 32:21 and Isa. 65:1-2).

"No people": The Gentiles. God would provoke the Jews to jealousy of the Gentiles who are not a part of Israel, God's special, chosen nation.

(Verses 20 and 21 are quotes from Isaiah 65:1-2).

Verses 1-16: In response to the prayer of the previous chapter, God speaks to the Gentiles who have come to trust in Him.

"I am found of them that sought me not" refers to the unconditional election of the Gentiles as the bulk of the New Testament church of God. (Romans 10:20).

While the Jews themselves are called *"rebellious people*, God still promises to bring a *"seed out of Jacob ... mine elect."*

The language here is reminiscent of Romans 11:1-5, where Paul insists that God has not forsaken His people, Israel.

The references to the plain of *"Sharon" and the "valley of Achor"*: blossoming abundantly look forward to the prosperity Israel will enjoy during the millennial kingdom.

Verses 1-7: In response to the prayer of (63:7-64:12), the Lord repeated the warning of His judgment.

Isaiah 65:1 "I am sought of them that asked not for me; I am found of them that sought me not: I said, behold me, behold me, unto a nation that was not called by my name."

"Asked not ... sought me not ... not called": Though Israel sought the Lord, they did so only hastily.

They did not genuinely seek Him. The New Testament assigns an additional sense to the words in Romans 10:20, applying them to Gentiles who find Him through the work of His sovereign grace.

This verse speaks of God coming to the Gentiles. Praise God!

All can be saved. We see the great mercy of God reaching beyond the physical house of Israel to all of mankind. God will now reveal Himself to the Gentiles.

We know that Jesus was accepted much more readily by the Gentiles than He was by the natural house of Israel. We see, in this verse, God reaching out to all mankind. The word *"behold"* is calling the nations to recognize God and come to Him.

Isaiah 65:2 "I have spread out my hands all day unto a rebellious people, which walk in a way that was not good, after their thoughts;"

The rebellious people of course are the natural house of Israel. God had been patient with them. He had reached out to them repeatedly. He had sent judges, and prophets, and even gave them His law, yet they rejected Him.

God had never left them, but they had left Him. They had committed spiritual adultery by seeking false gods. They were determined to walk in ways that were right in their sight, and not in the path God had given them.

Verses 3-4: Here Isaiah gave more references *to Israel's sins, such as defiance by practicing idolatry, communing with the spirits of the dead (a forbidden practice according to Deut. 18:10- 11), eating in ways forbidden by the Mosaic Law (Lev. 11:7-8), consuming food connected with idol sacrifices, and the arrogance of self-righteousness (Matt. 9:11; Luke 5:30; 18:11).*

Romans 10:21 "But to Israel he saith, all day long I have stretched forth my hands unto a disobedient and gainsaying people."

"Disobedient", means "to contradict" or *"to speak against."* As throughout her history, Israel once again contradicted the Word of God. This time it was the truth of the gospel.

Reference:

Spiritual Warfare Bible (2012) NKJV. Charisma House, Charisma Media / Charisma House Book Group. Lake Mary, Florida